LIFE IN
FORGIVENESS

LIFE IN
FORGIVENESS

Embracing
Reconciliation
with God
and Others

RICHARD T. CASE

©2013 by Richard T. Case

All rights reserved. No portion of this book may be reproduced, stored in a retrieval system, or transmitted in any form or by any means—electronic, mechanical, photocopy, recording, scanning, or other—except for brief quotations in critical reviews or articles, without the prior written permission of the publisher.

Originally published by Milestone Publishing House, Dallas/Fort Worth, Texas.

Currently published by Elevate Faith. A division of Elevate Publishing, Boise, Idaho.

Cover & Interior Design by Roy Roper, www.wideyedesign.net

All Scripture Quotations marked MSG are from The Message
© 1993, 1994, 1995, 1996, 2000, 2001, 2002 by Eugene H. Peterson.

All Scripture Quotations marked NIV are from THE HOLY BIBLE,
NEW INTERNATIONAL VERSION®, NIV®
© 1973, 1978, 1984, 2010 by Biblica, Inc.™ Used by permission. All rights reserved worldwide.

All Scripture quotations marked ESV are from the english standard version.
© 2001 by Crossway Bibles, a division of Good News Publishers.

All Scripture quotations marked KJV are from The King James Bible. Public Domain.

All Scripture quotations marked ASV are from NEW AMERICAN STANDARD BIBLE®.
© The Lockman Foundation 1960, 1962, 1963, 1968, 1971, 1972, 1973, 1975, 1977. Used by permission.

ISBN: 978-1-943425-42-6
Ebook ISBN: 978-1-943425-43-3

Printed in the USA

DEDICATION

I dedicate this book to my wonderful wife,
Linda. Over our 44 years of marriage,
she has demonstrated and lived out
"A Life in Forgiveness" and in doing so
has shown me the nature of God.
What a privilege and blessing this has been,
as we have together learned
what is true forgiveness and reconciliation.

CONTENTS

Acknowledgements ix
Foreword *by Richard Blackaby* XI
Introduction XIII

Chapter 1	Defining Moment	1
Chapter 2	Defining Unforgiveness	5
Chapter 3	Levels of Response	10
Chapter 4	Examining our Wounds	14
Chapter 5	Looking Beyond the Physical	22
Chapter 6	Fleshly Walkers	27
Chapter 7	Selfishness in Conflict	33
Chapter 8	Why We Withhold Forgiveness	42
Chapter 9	Defining Forgiveness	49
Chapter 10	God's Original Plan	55
Chapter 11	Our Failing and Falling	61
Chapter 12	Love's Victory	66
Chapter 13	Our Responsibility to Forgive	76
Chapter 14	Defining Reconciliation	81
Chapter 15	Truth of Separation	89
Chapter 16	Walking Hope for Wanderers	101
Chapter 17	Benefits of Reconciliation	105
Chapter 18	Calling to Reconcile	114
Chapter 19	Ministry of Reconciliation	124
Chapter 20	Practical Application Processing	132
Chapter 21	Questions and Answers	150

ACKNOWLEDGEMENTS

We are very grateful for our children – Peter & Shara (and their two sons, our grandsons – Joshua and Aidan), Michelle, and Christina & Mark (and their three daughters, our granddaughters – Nicole, Rachael and Riley). We so appreciate their love and support.

We wish to acknowledge The Blackabys, Henry and Richard, who have taught us such inspiring Biblical truth and how to deepen our experience with the Living God. Richard was kind enough to read the manuscript and offer suggestions for improvement and structuring. We so appreciate those who have walked with us over the years spiritually and encouraged us to spend time writing down what we were teaching - Tim & Mary Beth Sotos, Ken & Margie Blanchard, Tom & Barbara Crates, Randy & Linda Cain (our business partners) and special comrade Dave Dunkel. A special thanks to Melissa Loudermilk, who added much flavor to the manuscript and helped put it all together – a very gifted writer. Through her processing the truth of this book, she experienced a major breakthrough in forgiveness and reconciliation. Also, there are several co-laborers in Christ who have greatly contributed to helping us process the truth of forgiveness and reconciliation. First, our good friends and leaders with whom we are doing life together and are "giving it away" through our Living Waters Retreat Ministry - Lynda and Preston

LIFE IN FORGIVENESS

Pitts, Denny & Allyson Weinberg, Chris & Jacklyn Hoover, John and Michelle Santaferaro, Rick & Nancy Hoover, Blake & Marty Frye, Tom & Suzzane Ewing, Larry & Sherry Collett (with whom we are also working on writing projects together), Bob & Kerri Rockwell, Terry & Josephine Noetzel, Dirk & Cathy Davidson, Neal & Cathy Weisenberger, Chris & Heidi May, Scott & Terry Hitchcock, Rich & Mary Dillman, Scott & Kye Mitchell, Rich & Janet Cocchiaro, Ed and Becky Kobel, and Jake and Mary Beckel. Also, our good friends and associates involved with the CEO Forum – Mac & Karen McQuistion, Steve & Cheryl South, Steve & Nancy Menefee, Dick & Jackie Schultz, John & Wendy Beckett (who also encouraged us to write), Pat & Lauraine Caruana, Jeff & Lis Coors, Dave & Teri Fagin, Harold & Diane Smethills, Greg & Geri Brown, Mike & Cheryl Ducker, Chip & Jane Weisse, Jim & Ann Lindeman, Chuck & Roxy Morgan, Morrison & Kristen Carter, and Steve & Jennine Hoeft. Also, my Wednesday morning Bible group – Richard Andersen, Ken Blanchard, Phil Hodges, Esteen Lenyoun, Jim Mudd, Milt Richards, and Vince Siciliano. And finally, two couples who minister in Israel and have been such wonderful examples to us of expressing forgiveness and reconciliation in such a difficult place - Guy & Anita Kump, and Wayne & Ann Hilsden.

Our heartfelt thanks for and to all.

FOREWORD

One of the most sinister thieves in history continues to regularly rob vast numbers of people. This fiend is unforgiveness. It robs marriages of the joy and contentment intended by God. It alienates parents from their children and friends from one another. It divides churches and leads to generational blood feuds, and civil war. Yet despite having caused centuries of heartache, people still struggle to know how to forgive when someone hurts or disappoints them. That is why this book is so timely.

Rich Case is gifted to uniquely deal with this universal malady. He has helped numerous couples achieve the forgiveness and joy that had been elusive to them. He has helped CEOs, as well as church leaders, take their relationships to higher levels.

At last, Rich Case has delineated in print the biblical principles that have been setting people free for years. His practical applications and heartwarming stories will inspire you to strive for the relationships God intends for you to have. After reading this book, you will be inspired to hope that you, too, can experience forgiveness and reconciliation in even your most difficult relationships.

DR. RICHARD BLACKABY
President of Blackaby Ministries International
Author of *Experiencing God, The Seasons of God*

INTRODUCTION

Lack of forgiveness and reconciliation within relationships is an issue nearly all people experience. My wife, Linda, and I have been conducting marriage retreats for the past twelve years. In each retreat, almost all of the couples are dealing with these very issues: forgiveness and reconciliation. It often begins between the husband and wife but from there will often spill over into relationships with parents, siblings, children, friends, workers, bosses, etc. Why is this such a problem? Forgiving others is difficult, and the lack thereof is so incredibly epidemic. We are surrounded by selfish people who hurt and manipulate to obtain what they want. As we experience such wounds, frustrations and opposition, we naturally become angry and then struggle with what to do with the anger. It quickly turns into unforgiveness, and then hearts begin to harden and intimacy dissolves within relationships.

We maintain our unforgiveness, because the other party has not admitted or confessed their wrongdoing to us, so we wait on them to make things right. Since most people do not respond to conflict and wounds by resolving what they have done to us (and often fail to admit what we have done to them), everyone continues operating in unforgiveness. However, unforgiveness affects only our own soul and our own ability to enjoy life. As Linda and I have explored bringing healing to people's lives in this area of forgiveness, we have come to understand the primary reason it dominates almost all of our lives:

the great confusion between forgiveness and reconciliation. This book serves to explore the depths of these differences, offer biblical truths which allow us to live in forgiveness and then offer reconciliation to those around us. Furthermore, we will reveal how to maintain forgiveness when those around us are not willing to reconcile.

Case in point: at one of our retreats, a woman expressed deep bitterness toward her divorced father who had first oppressed her as a child and then rejected her as an adult. In fact, he had rejected the entire family! Along with her, all of her siblings were also estranged from their father . After helping her process through God's call to forgiveness and offer of reconciliation during the retreat, she sought the Word of God until she received the forgiveness towards her father she so eagerly desired. Having experienced the release of forgiving her father, she wanted to share it with the rest of her family. So she called each of her siblings and expressed to them the freedom she had so beautifully received. She even went further and suggested each sibling work through the same process until they, too, fully embraced and received the same forgiveness God was calling them to accept and extend. However, all of her siblings declined and chose to remain enslaved to their bitterness. Choosing bitterness and refusing to forgive actually places one in bondage, causing much pain and angst. This consequence could fully be avoided, as we will see throughout this book.

But wait … her story continues. After this precious lady had forgiven her father, she then contacted him to offer reconciliation. Her father was pleased to hear from her and was willing to meet. Though he was not able to fully understand much of her hurt, they did reconcile at a surface level and each experienced and felt the freedom of having

INTRODUCTION

regained a lost relationship. Then, less than a week later, her father passed away. This dear lady praised God for having not only having received the truth and revelation of forgiveness and the freedom it brought her, but also having had the opportunity and power to express her love to her father before he died. And yet, to this very day, her siblings now have an element of bitterness towards their sister, because she was the only one of them who had contact with their father in his final days. They continue to be burdened by the bitterness they have developed over the years, and now that bitterness cannot be let go. Again, this book will show how we each can come to, receive and welcome the forgiveness of those who have hurt us, even those who have passed away and reconciliation seems impossible.

Unfortunately, this woman's story is not unique. Most of us have similar stories in our own lives and are living within various levels of unforgiveness and with the roots of bitterness growing towards those around us. As we will discover, the truth and revelation of God found in the Scriptures declares God's call to us. It's a call to forgive, and forgive 100% of the time. In the same way, He desires us to live in utter and complete freedom all the time as well, which can only be obtained through forgiveness. We will also learn that forgiveness does not equal reconciliation, because reconciliation takes two willing parties. While this is very complicated at the onset, we can understand the simplicity of our position in the reconciliation process – which always starts and ends with forgiveness.

CHAPTER 1
DEFINING MOMENT

After being married for forty-three years, Linda and I can say from experience how critical it is to live in a constant state of forgiveness in a marriage. We had many opportunities to learn this during our first decade of being man and wife. Though both of my parents have passed on to be with Christ, they shaped who I am, how I interact with others, and how I was introduced to the Father. I grew up in a professional home – my father was a surgeon and my mother a socialite. Even though my father was very generous and taught me great wisdom about how to appropriately approach life with all of its challenges and every-day issues, he was mostly absent. My mother, on the other hand, was very dominant in controlling the family, which included five children. In fact, her domineering approach through anger, physical force and verbal demands were often irrational. Being a good athlete, I spent most of my time outside the school playing ball (football, basketball, baseball) just like nearly every other kid did in Indiana during that time. Participating in sports allowed me a frequent and welcome escape from the irrational domination and allowed me to receive much needed praise and personal affirmation from coaches and fellow teammates. To couple my natural athleticism, I had a personality such that I was willing to go to battle and fight things through to a tidy conclusion. However, I quickly learned the battle with my mother was simply not winnable. So, what strategy did

LIFE IN FORGIVENESS

I use to survive? A complicated and cyclical one: 1.) Go to battle; 2.) Inevitably lose the battle; 3.) Ignore the conflict entirely; 4.) Figure out how to function independently until the next battle arose.

You see, being faced with the enigma of being a part of a family highly dominated by my mother but still living with much practical freedom was my life. My parents were often too busy to really pay any attention to what I was doing or where I was, and yet, I was fully expected (and managed) to stay out of trouble to ensure I would neither create problems for my parents nor myself. I accomplished high marks in school, married my high school sweetheart, Linda, during our undergraduate years and then graduated with an MBA from the University of Southern California. All good accomplishments, but families still can cause tension even amongst the proudest of achievements. After the completion of my MBA and receiving my first "real" job, Linda and I both became followers of Christ, and God blessed us with our first daughter. Despite our happiness and joy, my mother caused us much heartache and problems, although we lived in separate states. Angry phone calls, harsh words towards and regarding Linda, and being treated with indignation and irrational behavior when we visited all became our normal and almost expected interactions with her over the years. Then, it all came to the breaking point one holiday when our family – then consisting of three children – visited my now divorced parents. We basically spent the entire festive occasion angry and frustrated. My mother screamed at our children, and each and every person was tense. To say we were unhappy would be an understatement.

We left Indiana and vowed that we had had enough, and any contact

DEFINING MOMENT

with them would cease to exist. I was angry, and Linda was angry; we were hurt, and our children were hurt. We decided we wanted our holidays with our children to be joyful and fun, not difficult and hurtful. That was it – we were done – our decision had been made. We stopped accepting my mother's calls and had absolutely no contact for a few months. And yet, the lack of communication merely made my mother more irrational than ever. Her behavior and "guilt trips" escalated, only to get us back to a position where she could dominate us once again. None of her behavior made us want to reconcile, in fact, it solidified the idea of keeping the relationship in "stand-off" mode. However, we noticed something … our hearts were being held captive by the continued anger, frustration, and harshness. Our heart "issue" did not just remain confined to my mom either. It spilled over into all of our other relationships, and we were seemingly always on edge and jumpy. However, God had mercy on us and used our pastor to change our hearts. He delivered a sermon one Sunday on how God commands forgiveness, regardless of what someone has done to us, virtually unpacking the truths contained within Ephesians 4:25–32. His words really struck Linda and I both collectively and individually in our spirits. So we agreed to explore together what the Lord had to say regarding forgiveness in light of what was going on with my mother. After about a month of soaking in the Word, we finally understood that Christ did not only freely give forgiveness to us, but we also are commanded to live in this forgiveness all the time with all people. Equally as important, we realized also that forgiveness is not the same as reconciliation.

LIFE IN FORGIVENESS

We both were able to receive complete forgiveness regarding my mother and immediately received the freedom that accompanies that forgiveness in our lives. Yes, we understood my mom would never sit down and discuss all the things she had done to hurt me during my childhood, to hurt us during our dating and then marriage relationship, or even what she had done to our children. However, we were able to establish reconciliation with her, albeit small. That reconciliation also required us to establish certain boundaries, like not celebrating holidays together. This would ensure that we could all enjoy each other's company over the remaining years we had together, which we were able to enjoy. We no longer let her irrational anger bother us and chose to no longer join her battles. Because we refused to join the battles, our times together became more sweet and pleasant. More importantly, our lives were never again held captive or identified by the roots of bitterness we so tightly held toward her; thus, we enjoyed the freedom of forgiveness through Christ's work and Christ working within us. You could say this turn of events defined our lives. Since then, Linda and I have continued exercising this amazing truth with all our relationships and continue to live in the very same all-encompassing freedom. Having served as pastors of various churches, and over the past twelve years conducting spiritual renewal retreats, we fully understand almost everyone struggles with the issue of unforgiveness. We have all been hurt by people, and the extent of the bondage can overshadow us. The resolution to the issue is really not to confront and merely amend what others have done to us, but to not let others' actions, regardless of what they may be, ruin our souls and keep us in captivity.

CHAPTER 2
DEFINING UNFORGIVENESS

When we look at Linda's and my journey, which led to that pivotal decision to not only forgive my mother but also to apply forgiveness to all of our relationships, it leads most people we come in contact with to question whether they are operating in unforgiveness. They wonder what does it look like. Exactly what is unforgiveness?

What is "Unforgiveness"?

"Do not grieve the Holy Spirit of God, by whom you were sealed for the day of redemption. Let all bitterness and wrath and anger and clamor and slander be put away from you, along with all malice. Be kind to one another, tender-hearted, forgiving each other, just as God in Christ also has forgiven you." Ephesians 4:30–32

"And just as they did not see fit to acknowledge God any longer, God gave them over to a depraved mind, to do those things which are not proper, being filled with all unrighteousness, wickedness, greed, evil; full of envy, murder, strife, deceit, malice; they are gossips, slanderers, haters of God, insolent, arrogant, boastful, inventors of evil, disobedient to parents, without understanding, untrustworthy, unloving, unmerciful; and although they know the ordinance of

LIFE IN FORGIVENESS

God, that those who practice such things are worthy of death, they not only do the same, but also give hearty approval to those who practice them." Romans 1:28–32

"Now the deeds of the flesh are evident, which are: immorality, impurity, sensuality, idolatry, sorcery, enmities, strife, jealousy, outbursts of anger, disputes, dissensions, factions, envying, drunkenness, carousing, and things like these, of which I forewarn you, just as I have forewarned you, that those who practice such things will not inherit the kingdom of God." Galatians 5:19–21

Unforgiveness, simply put, is the absence of forgiveness. The absence of forgiveness in a person's life allows chaos and evil character traits to run amuck. Where there is no forgiveness, there is no trace of anything resembling either a forgiven life, forgiveness of others, or the evidence of Christ.

So, why the emphasis on the bitterness, wrath, and slander caused by unforgiveness? Each of these reactions deeply grieves the heart of a holy God, and since we serve a triune God, such actions also grieve the Holy Spirit. We are called to abhor such actions and instead embrace those attributes, which reflect God Himself, such as tenderness, mercy, and kindness. We are to do these things out of a grateful heart, forgiving others because we have been forgiven. However, we do live in an evil world, full of people who do evil things, and God has given them up to be ruled by their own corrupted minds. Corrupted minds cannot do anything else but hate their creator, stir up strife, cultivate deception, and heartily approve of anyone else who does so. Those

DEFINING UNFORGIVENESS

who walk according to the flesh and those who walk in the Spirit are completely and utterly different, in fact, opposite. Those who love God are robed with His righteousness, and their hearts overflow with mercy, humbleness, and truth. Yet, to be honest, even Christians sometimes participate in one or more of the litany of actions described in Galatians. If Christians have the Spirit of the living and loving God residing within them, why do we sometimes act so contrarily?

Simply put, we do not forgive. Unforgiveness lies at the roots of bitterness, wrath, anger, and slander. When our hearts are wounded by circumstances or people who hurt or manipulate us, we sometimes choose to hold on to anger and refuse to forgive. We remain in the pool of anger and animosity, and we act out accordingly. For some reason we have chosen to hold on to our wounds, the bitterness, and our hurt in lieu of forgiving and moving on. What we are unaware of is the action of withholding forgiveness imprisons our hearts and souls. It keeps us from living by the Spirit and, in turn, keeps us enslaved to anger, which consequently leads to bitterness. The longer we withhold forgiveness, the more difficult it becomes to offer love, mercy and kindness to others or to receive it ourselves. Yet, making a conscious decision to just not get angry doesn't work. We are unable in our own power to resolve our anger or to naturally forgive. Unfortunately for us, the process of anger leading to unforgiveness happens automatically. We cannot escape its natural progression. Read the following Scriptures:

> *"Be angry, and yet do not sin; do not let the sun go down on your anger, and do not give the devil an opportunity."* Ephesians 4:26–27

LIFE IN FORGIVENESS

> *"Therefore thus says the Lord God, 'Behold, I am laying in Zion a stone, a tested stone, a costly cornerstone for the foundation, firmly placed. He who believes in it will not be disturbed. I will make justice the measuring line and righteousness the level; then hail will sweep away the refuge of lies and the waters will overflow the secret place.'"* Isaiah 28:16–17

We should start out by being encouraged here. Scripture clearly states that it is okay and perfectly acceptable to be angry. Anger is a natural and God-given emotion. In fact God himself experiences anger! We were given this natural emotion so that our sense of right and wrong, reality and truth, and our everyday lives collide in a beautiful symphony. However, there is a line drawn in the sand – be angry and do not sin. How is this possible? Check all unresolved anger. If we let our anger, hurt, or feelings of betrayal fester, we give the enemy an opportunity to affect us, affect our lives, and affect our relationship with God and others. We cannot prevent getting angry, because we cannot prevent the circumstances, which cause anger in the first place; but we need to know our response to such instances can lead to sin. Sin, simply explained, is to miss the mark. It's an archery term. If you have ever watched an archery event or even attempted the sport, you know the archer is always aiming for the center of their target, right? This is their mark. When they hit it, everyone cheers, and they feel a great sense of accomplishment. But when they miss their mark, the miss is called a sin. It is the same way in our spiritual lives. We miss our mark each and every time we maintain our anger and continue down the treacherous path of unforgiveness, instead of processing through

DEFINING UNFORGIVENESS

our hurt, which leads to forgiveness. It is this very unwillingness to forgive which allows the devil a foothold in our lives, causing wounds to deepen into hardness of heart, bitterness, wrath, etc.

But let's not stop here; let's look further. The cornerstone of our faith is Jesus. This cornerstone is unique and is the foundation of true faith. This stone has been created by the tools of justice and righteousness, and thus, made perfect. We know that God acts and reacts justly and operates righteously when it comes to our wounds. Justice is, and always has been, God's measuring line. It's the mark for which He is aiming. So, if justice is God's mark and we have the indwelling of God's spirit, it is natural for us to react with anger to unfairness, wrongdoing, and inequality. Again, this anger is sanctioned by God and has been established as his measuring line automatically dictating our responses. Take a moment to sit back and think about the anger in your own life. What are you angry about? At whom are you angry? What did they do to you? What did they deny you? At what injustices in the world are you infuriated? Take a good introspective account of your own heart and its hurts, which have resulted in anger. Write them down if you need to, and then look at the results of the conflicts. You will probably notice that your response to being angry differs with each circumstance, and the relationships are strained at various levels. This is a good thing to notice. Remember, our goal should be to not continue with the way things are. It is to apply the healing balm of forgiveness to each and every circumstance, as a way to not only release the bitterness and anger but to also allow the fullness of Christ's work to manifest its complete power within you.

CHAPTER 3
LEVELS OF RESPONSE

We encounter unjust circumstances or people causing injustice every day. The anger and frustration that accompanies each event is unique to the people associated with it and to the offense that occurred. In our experience, we have noticed that there are basically three differing levels at which humanity typically responds to wounds. These are: Minimal, Partial, and Complete. Let's take a look at each one.

1. **Minimal Response:** You have been wounded. Things like this happen nearly every day, but at the minimal level, you can be upset and even notice a strain on the relationship but not much more. You do not withdraw from your offender or from the hurt experienced and do not act harshly towards them. You are still able to politely talk with them and even be in the same room. Yet, when you do converse, the dialogue tends to be rather short and curt with a slight edge to it. The distance between the two of you can be sensed and you two may act differently or dogmatically towards each other. For instance, let's say you have lunch with a friend but they were a no-show with no warning or explanation. When you email them later that day to find out what happened, they simply respond with, "I just got too busy … sorry." Your immediate

LEVELS OF RESPONSE

response is to get a bit miffed that they didn't show enough common courtesy to at least call or text message to cancel. Even though this is a minimal response to the conflict, you still wrestle with the fact that they don't consider the event as being disrespectful to you or your friendship. You may not be holding a grudge, but the relationship still feels slightly strained, which was not previously experienced. As a result of your minimal withdrawal, your friend also withdraws in response, and the strain continues to be felt and will potentially deepen if left unresolved or ignored.

2. **Partial Response:** You have been wounded, but this time it is a different circumstance and there has been an initial separation between you and the one who hurt you. Typically, your reaction would be to not talk about or deal with the issue at hand but still be clearly and noticeably angry. At this level, you want nothing to do with your offender, even if you know you must interact with them at a later date. The conflict clearly affects your ability to relate to them on a friendly or even rational level. Many times you may suppress your feelings, which only harms the relationship further instead of resolving the issue at hand. Your relationship is obviously strained, and the two of you interact with great indifference, but this indifference and strained relationship becomes the new normal for you. Here is a possible scenario to clarify: You are an active member of your church and currently serve on a committee. Another person on the same committee complains to a third

party that you are not pulling your weight and often have poor ideas. When you finally hear about what has been said, you become angry and defensive but don't want to confront your opponent. So, what do you do? You find excuses to not show up to the committee meetings (to avoid seeing them) and when you do see them, there is an overwhelming indifference tainted with loathing towards them. Even when he or she speaks, you fail to join in any of the discussions, making sure your silence is noticed and felt. It is obvious to others, not to mention the two of you directly, that the relationship is seriously strained; but neither of you wish to resolve the conflict. In response to the issue as a whole, your anxiety increases greatly whenever you think of going to a committee meeting, and you no longer enjoy participating with any of the work done through the group. The conflict has lost you a friend and the joy associated with working with your church.

3. **Complete Response:** Yet again, you are hurt, but this stage is by far the most severe. You want no contact – absolutely nothing to do with the one who harmed you. All communication between the two of you has ceased. You are clearly and noticeably mad and have resolutely decided that unless your offender apologizes and admits they were wrong, reconciliation will not happen. At this stage, nothing will make you change your mind either.. Here's an example: you and a Christian friend got into a heated argument, which resulted in them walking out and slamming the door in your face. Your friend

LEVELS OF RESPONSE

has neither called to discuss the issue, nor to discuss anything, for that matter. In response, you refuse to communicate either. Since you are completely convinced they are the one who owes you an apology, the relationship is broken and any association with them personally (whether through church or work) is ardently avoided.

Do you remember when it was suggested for you to take an account of the anger in your own life? Revisit those circumstances. Before we progress any further, please be willing to go deeper. Has there been anyone in your life you have cut off communication with entirely? Who was it? What caused the separation? Be also willing to admit your own contribution to the situation. Is there anyone with whom you used to be friends? What happened to make you now indifferent towards each other? Can you even remember? Please spend some time praying with the Father to reveal to you more areas in your past and present that need His healing touch of forgiveness. Will it hurt to revisit painful times? Yes, but it is worth every tear you shed, if it leads to true and complete healing. Do not be afraid or too stubborn to look into the darkest recesses of your heart. Swing those doors you refuse to open to others wide open to Jesus. Allow Him full access to your heart and mind, and He will be faithful to not only reveal the places, memories and circumstances He wants to heal, but He WILL heal them if you just let Him.

CHAPTER 4
EXAMINING OUR WOUNDS

If you are like most people, you probably have an incredibly long list of harmful actions and words done and said to you through the years. Unfortunately, this is not uncommon in today's world, but with the litany of wounds we experience, what necessitates the level at which we respond? Everything has to do with your wound: how it happened, by whom it happened, etc. The events which surround your hurt, everything about its environment contributes to how we respond.

1. **First, what is the severity of the hurt?** If a wound or frustration occurs and it is temporal or nominal in nature, a minimal response will typically ensue. For example, you are at a restaurant and the waitress is not as attentive as you would like (you have needed a refill for ten minutes, you are still waiting for some utensils, etc.) or messes up your order (you ordered the grilled chicken with broccoli and received fried chicken with fries). So, you naturally respond in anger. However, because you know the interaction is merely temporary and have no real relationship with the waitress, your response is usually minimal. In the grand scheme of life, this interaction matters little and you will not have an ongoing level of unforgiveness. On the other hand, if your mother calls

incessantly making you feel guilty for not visiting enough, the severity of your wound may be quite strong. Why the difference? There are two reasons: 1.) you have a deep and ongoing relationship with your mother, and 2.) the actions are continually being experienced. In this case, your response more than likely will move to the partial or complete level, depending on the harshness experienced. This and the next item – frequency of hurt – was what contributed to the partial and then the complete break in the relationship with my mother. It was personal; the words were very severe; and it happened over and over again. Therefore, it became increasingly difficult to let any jab or snide remark go unnoticed or ignored. As a result, our response shifted from partial strain (avoiding being together as much as possible) to complete strain (withdrawing completely and avoiding all contact).

2. **What is the frequency of the hurt?** If you are wounded once, and if it is a single event, your response tends to be minimal (you are not given credit for all of your contribution to a collaborative work presentation, but it had never happened before). However, if the wound happens repetitively, your response will move to a partial and/or complete one. Let's say you have designated Sunday afternoon as your Sabbath for you and your family. You have politely asked friends and family to respect that by not calling during that time.

Now, if your relatives repeatedly ignore your request and

continue to call you on Sunday afternoons, the frequency of the offense will increase the level of response.

3. **What is your current level of frustration in other areas?** It is these "other" areas that typically lead to further disappointment in life, steering you towards withholding forgiveness. Your response to all frustrating circumstances can be triggered, or your responses intensified, by your own emotional state as it relates to the other areas in your life:

   a. **Tired, weary** - if an individual is worn out, they tend to be more sensitive; their emotions more easily heightened, and thus, can quickly shift from anger to unforgiveness, even regarding circumstances that would normally be deemed trifling.

   b. **Worried, anxious** - if one is experiencing worry and anxiety, opposition intensifies these emotions and again will quickly trigger deeper levels of unforgiveness.

   c. **Fear** - if anyone lives in a general state of fear or are afraid of future outcomes, resistance in particular areas may have a more significant impact. Fear is tied to many other emotions and can quickly trigger the deeper emotional roots that lead to unforgiveness.

   d. **Roots of bitterness, anger** – anyone's current level of anger and/or bitterness will only serve to intensify new wounds and opposition. Other circumstances will be seen as added frustrations and will further create a sense of injustice in a wounded person's life.

e. **Grief, sadness** - if someone is experiencing grief due to loss or disappointing events, new hurtful experiences in their lives can serve as a catalyst for deeper levels of grief, again leading to unforgiveness.

f. **Disappointments, resignation** – if an individual has tried unsuccessfully to overcome obstacles in their life as a way to deal with those who have hurt them, they can live in a perpetual state of disappointment or resignation.

All of these, alone or together, can intensify our responses to any hurtful circumstance. Linda and I have found that this is a great scheme the enemy uses – various terse conditions, which create strained relationships and intensify our feelings of unforgiveness. Let's take a very practical and real example: If I come home from work tired and weary, plus anxious and disappointed about things not going well at work, it is easy for me to overreact when Linda didn't do something I asked her to do. Uncharacteristically, I snap at her which leads to her snapping back, since my overreaction was out of line. Thus, begins the edginess and a very slippery slope towards unforgiveness. Before we learned the importance of forgiveness and reconciliation, we would not have dealt with this type of situation at all, much less in a constructive manner. The result of not dealing with situations such as this is each of us carries around low levels of anger, which then erupts inappropriately and unexpectedly during various scenarios. Consequently, roots of bitterness developed toward each other and the relationship continued to become more and more strained. When either I failed to fulfill her desires or she failed mine, eruptions in anger became commonplace and the intensity of the strain in our relationship progressively deepened. Normal situations that most people typically overlook became sources of irritation, frustration, and continued overreaction.

4. **What is the hardness and/or stubbornness of the offending person?** The way in which you react is directly dictated by the way your offender acts towards you. If the one who has hurt you acts harshly and in a very difficult manner, your response level increases. If your offender is stubborn and not willing to process through the hurtful action with you, your response level tends to increase. If the one hurting you continues operating in their pride and self-centeredness, then your response tends to immediately lean more toward a partial or complete separation. This was a big contributor to my anger and unforgiveness toward my mother. Throughout my life she had had an extremely harsh and stubborn way about her. In no uncertain terms, were we told it was either her way or the highway. So even when she did have legitimate things to challenge me on, my defenses were permanently up because of the regular verbal battles and power plays I had

experienced with and by her in the past. Though I live in forgiveness and freedom today, still when someone harshly confronts me, I have an initial negative reaction. I recognize that this is because of all the years I experienced the same treatment by my mother.

5. **Is there an emotional escalation of the moment?** Your own emotions can escalate within the conflict and the moment, depending on which emotions are triggered and how you are being treated. For example:

    a. **Words spoken that accuse and/or attack one's character** - if the wounded party is falsely or harshly accused, such an attack of their character would only deepen their response. In the heat of arguments, it is easy for us to use words that hurt and wound others. We often say things that accuse others and attack their character, which results in unnecessary wounds. In our early years of marriage, Linda and I frequently used such words as "you always", and "you never" when we argued. These words, spawned from our anger and falsely flung at each other, directly attacked the other's character and were only used to try and win the battle. By using these words and allowing the roots of bitterness and unforgiveness to deepen, it became easier and easier to use character assassination the next time around, just to hurt the other person or even to harm a beloved spouse.

b. Circumstances that appear to deepen hurt and anger - such circumstances could either be imagined or real. If someone believes that the people opposing them are doing it purposely or callously, whether real or perceived, it can deepen their response to the conflict. This is another great trick of the enemy. We often see this as well during our retreats. We had one couple where the husband stated inadvertently within the group that he was looking to start a new business. This was news to the wife! With the bombshell given at the retreat, she had assumed her husband had already decided to quit his job and start a new business, without even talking to or discussing it with her. As a result, she withdrew from her husband, and Linda and I could clearly see on the second day of the retreat their relationship was strained a bit. We called them together and helped them process and verbalize what each was feeling. When the wife stated she was fearful her husband was starting a new business, the husband responded that it was just a fleeting thought and that he hadn't even given it any serious consideration at all! The wife's initial reaction was a false perception, but to her it was real. A comment or a supposed circumstance can be interpreted in many ways, and if its interpretation causes fear, anxiety or worry, then it can easily go to anger and frustration. This is why it is so critical to continually communicate and make sure there is full understanding

EXAMINING OUR WOUNDS

and agreement on what is being stated and not to let any circumstance or inadvertent comments throw off our relationships.

Go back to your list of wounds, anger and broken relationships. This time take each situation, and honestly assess whether there were extenuating circumstances that elevated your response. Had you been up all night with a sick child? Did your spouse just get diagnosed with cancer? Was your character being attacked? Were you being yelled at or belittled? Was it the forty-ninth time your father brought it up? What is going on in your life right now? If you know finances are extremely tight, and you are worried about making the mortgage payment, just know you will have the tendency to overreact to any slight aggravation. Knowing where you are and taking into account the environment of the conflict will help us not only more clearly understand our role in the conflict, but it will also allow a greater level of healing to take place.

CHAPTER 5
LOOKING BEYOND THE PHYSICAL

The information given regarding the levels at which we typically respond to hurt and frustration in our lives is important to know. Also valuable to note is how our responses are triggered by our past and by others. But these deal only with the physical realm. We must also address how the spiritual realm affects us and how quickly we forgive and process through the hurt inflicted upon us. The levels at which we react to our wounds and how long we remain in our anger is directly related to both our and our offender's current walk with God. As you read through the following scriptures, consider the following example and the various possible responses within this scenario. Consider a couple who has been married for 10 years, has done well financially, has three children, and are active churchgoers. Five years ago the husband decided to purchase a condo in the city for his parents so that they would have a nice home. The parents had initially agreed to pay the monthly mortgage amount, and at the time of purchase, the down payment on the condo was not a strain on the couple's finances. While there was not initial unity and complete discussion of the purchase, the real estate transaction had not been a source of major conflict for the couple. However, the parents got into a financial bind and stopped paying the monthly mortgage. The payments then became the responsibility of this couple. For a while everything was okay, but then the couple experienced a significant reduction in income due to a fluctuating economy. All of a sudden, this added monthly expense became a major strain on their budget and relationship. Because of the obligation felt by the husband to his parents, he refused to discuss any attempt to make budget changes, regardless of its necessity. This resulted in a partial level of unforgiveness and further strained the relationship with his wife. Using this example, let's see how different scenarios can play out.

1. **Walking in the Spirit:** Just because we are walking in the Spirit, does not mean we will avoid being angry. Remember when we spoke about God being angry and how anger was a natural emotion given to us? Remember the scripture telling us to be angry but not to sin in our anger? When we walk in the spirit, there will be times when righteous anger presents itself because of an injustice done or us having been wronged. However, here the wound is acknowledged, but the responding level returns to the minimal stage. Read the following Scriptures:

"Let love be without hypocrisy. Abhor what is evil; cling to what is good. Be devoted to one another in brotherly love; give preference to one another in honor; not lagging behind in diligence, fervent in spirit, serving the Lord; rejoicing in hope, persevering in tribulation, devoted to prayer, contributing to the needs of the saints, practicing hospitality. Bless those who persecute you; bless and do not curse. Rejoice with those who rejoice, and weep with those who weep. Be of the same mind toward one another; do

not be haughty in mind, but associate with the lowly. Do not be wise in your own estimation. Never pay back evil for evil to anyone. Respect what is right in the sight of all men. If possible, so far as it depends on you, be at peace with all men. Never take your own revenge, beloved, but leave room for the wrath of God, for it is written, 'Vengeance is Mine, I will repay,' says the Lord. 'But if your enemy is hungry, feed him, and if he is thirsty, give him a drink; for in so doing you will heap burning coals on his head.' Do not be overcome by evil, but overcome evil with good."
Romans 12:9–21

Those who choose to follow Christ are called to walk as Christ did - to love God and love one another. You know you truly love someone else, when you are at peace with them and fully allow God to hit His "mark" and enact His justice, in His own time and way. Yet, we who are Christians are told to go farther. We are even told to care for the needs of our enemies, to feed them and give them something to drink. We are commanded to repay evil with good, which is much easier said than done. However, if both parties involved in a conflict are actively walking in the Spirit, then they will both seek peace and reconciliation. They will each realize that justice is indeed served by God, and there is no need to maintain unforgiveness or to repay evil with evil. Rather, both parties will see the good in the situation and the good in each other. There will be a desire and willingness to work through any hurt and disagreement, as well as the mutual goal of obtaining a God solution, meaning seeking God's will for this difficult situation. Therefore, the level of unforgiveness will remain at a minimal level. Their relationship will eventually return to full release and reconciliation, because they have fully recognized and embraced the heart of God wanting to bring healing and freedom to their conflict. They will continue to respect and honor each other – until a resolution is achieved – resulting in restoration of peace and joy in the relationship, as well as complete freedom and intimacy.

In our case study, if the husband were walking in the spirit, he would not shut down the concerns of his wife. Rather, he would openly accept them and begin communication to understand the facts of the situation from her perspective and then would be willing to discuss how God can provide a solution to the dilemma. Harsh words and tribulation would play no part in this, only a willingness to continue to talk and pray until God presented a solution. Neither the husband nor the wife would hold on to any anger, roots of bitterness or allow the situation to be "off limits."

2. **Walking in Selfishness:** when one or both parties of a conflict are not walking in the Spirit, they are walking in selfishness, otherwise known as the flesh. When that happens, the response to a wound will be on an either partial or complete level and, unfortunately, it will become very normal for that level of unforgiveness to remain there. So, what is selfishness or how can we identify it? Selfishness is defined as

exercising your self-will (doing what you want to do), being self-centered (always having only your best interest at heart), and exercising your self-agenda (what is going to bring you the most happiness and prosperity). When either or both parties involved in a conflict desire their own will, focus on their own personal desires, and have only their own agenda at heart, the goal will never be to release unforgiveness. Rather, the goal is always to maintain withholding forgiveness in order to manipulate the other person, the situation as a whole, and to ultimately achieve their desired outcome. Now this is not always the case. Sometimes, as you may have noticed in your own experience, the resistance to forgiveness may only be one-sided. You may be doing everything right – walking in the Spirit, but even though you may be, the other party may be walking in selfishness. If so, be forewarned. Just know their desire to live peaceably and release their self-centeredness is low, and they will continue to maintain the hurt, opposition and frustration that serve their purposes. An integral part of gaining the freedom associated with receiving and extending forgiveness is to be honest with God and ourselves. How often are you and I truly walking in the Spirit? Think of all the times you experienced hurt and conflict arose. How many of those times were you walking in the Spirit? Are you walking in the Spirit now? How do you know if you are walking in the Spirit, versus walking and operating in the flesh? This is a good question, to which God has given us answers.

CHAPTER 6
FLESHLYWALKERS

As we stated before, we need to be able to recognize where we are coming from – spiritually speaking, that is. However, we need also to assess from where our offenders are coming, so we can proceed with wisdom. So, what do people walking in selfishness look like? Let's go to God's Word to find out:

An unbeliever, operating without the Spirit of God:

"Therefore, just as through one man sin entered into the world, and death through sin, and so death spread to all men, because all sinned." Romans 5:12

"For all have sinned and fall short of the glory of God." Romans 3:23

"For the wrath of God is revealed from heaven against all ungodliness and unrighteousness of men who suppress the truth in unrighteousness, because that which is known about God is evident within them; for God made it evident to them. For since the creation of the world His invisible attributes, His eternal power and divine nature, have been clearly seen, being understood through what has been made, so that they are without excuse. For even though they knew God, they did not honor Him as God or give thanks, but they became futile in their speculations, and their foolish heart was darkened. Professing to be wise, they became fools,

and exchanged the glory of the incorruptible God for an image in the form of corruptible man and of birds and four-footed animals and crawling creatures. Therefore God gave them over in the lusts of their hearts to impurity, so that their bodies would be dishonored among them. For they exchanged the truth of God for a lie, and worshiped and served the creature rather than the Creator, who is blessed forever. Amen." Romans 1:18–25

Sin and selfishness impact everyone. As stated in the Word, all have sinned and fallen short of God's standard of perfection. In addition, his wrath is shown to those who do not worship the one true God and who squelch the truth and participate in ungodly and unrighteous acts. Unbelievers do not have the spirit of God living in them, so then, why should it surprise any of us that unbelievers operate in anything other than selfishness? Without God's Spirit, they are completely self-centered, absorbed in self-will and operate only within their own self-agenda. It is impossible for them to act otherwise. Because of this, they will naturally give little thought to seeking peace with others – rather, they will typically use emotional manipulation to obtain selfish desires, regardless of how it affects or hurts others, even loved ones.

A believer, operating carnally, in the Flesh:

"For those who are according to the flesh set their minds on the things of the flesh, but those who are according to the Spirit, the things of the Spirit. For the mind set on the flesh is death, but the mind set on the Spirit is life and peace, because the mind set on the flesh is hostile toward God; for it does not subject itself to the

law of God, for it is not even able to do so, and those who are in the flesh cannot please God." Romans 8:5-8

"But if you have bitter jealousy and selfish ambition in your heart, do not be arrogant and so lie against the truth. This wisdom is not that which comes down from above, but is earthly, natural, and demonic. For where jealousy and selfish ambition exist, there is disorder and every evil thing. But the wisdom from above is first pure, then peaceable, gentle, reasonable, full of mercy and good fruits, unwavering, without hypocrisy. And the seed whose fruit is righteousness is sown in peace by those who make peace." James 3:14–18

Believers are different than unbelievers – literally as different as night and day, dark and light, and life and death. We have a choice in how to live and approach conflict. According to Romans, we can choose to either walk in the Spirit or in the flesh. Those who choose to walk according to the flesh have chosen to be ruled by self (self-will, self-agenda, etc.). Those who walk accordingly are arrogant, jealous, and their lives are in general disorder and full of evil. However, Christians who choose to live by the Spirit are peaceable, gentle, and the list continues. One vital point to internalize is that our human nature dictates we do not have a neutral choice in these matters (see Romans 7: 13 – 24). Rather, we naturally default to walking in the flesh and in self, when we fail to choose to walk according to the Spirit. When we are governed by a carnal mind and are satisfying our flesh, there are three natural consequences: death of the Spirit (where we quench the

LIFE IN FORGIVENESS

Spirit, as if it were dead, and refuse to allow it to operate within and enliven us), enmity against God (where we work directly against the purposes and will of God), and when we are completely unable to please God. Consequently, maintaining unforgiveness becomes easy when our flesh is dominant and these consequences are running rampant in our lives. Our flesh desires to maintain unforgiveness, so we can, in turn, manipulate others to achieve our objectives. In essence we want what we want when we want it, and we will do what is needed to get it. We may also continue to withhold forgiveness in order to foster a constant victim mentality, which is also a foothold of the enemy. Regardless, in any of these instances where we remain in our anger, we are continually subjecting ourselves to further hurt and oppression by others.

In our earlier example, the husband continues to keep the issue of parental housing "off limits." Whenever the wife suggests they discuss finances and budgets, the husband automatically knows where the conversation is heading and shuts her down immediately. He repeatedly says he has "everything under control" and "everything will be fine," but such is not the case. In actuality fear and anxiety only increase, because the couple is not making their ends meet. The husband only gets increasingly concerned about failure and worries further about the future, not to mention refusing to address a big portion of the problem, which is his parents' situation, is also a nagging concern. He has found himself in a catch-22, or what's considered a classic double bind. He has no solution. Any resolution he thinks of is inevitably going to cause further stress and strain, so he results in believing no discussion is better than confrontation any day. In the meantime, his wife mirrors his own fears and concerns. After she is faced with the loss of her disposable income, she now spends strictly on needs for the children, but she swallows her anger and emotions knowing that the subject is "off limits." She uses the credit card to make purchases for the family and just endures her husband's angry outbursts when they inevitably come. All too soon, the ever-increasing strain and consequent edginess characterizes their relationship, and it becomes their new normal. In this situation, both the husband and the wife are acting selfishly. Although the husband's selfishness, avoidance, and anger are easily identified, the wife's response is just as selfish. She avoids the entire issue for the same reason. She merely wants to protect herself, while avoiding the conflict entirely. If either of them were actually walking in the Spirit as opposed to the flesh, they would pray and then be willing to open up with full disclosure to discuss all the facts. If the initial attempt to resolve the conflict was not received, then a third party would be needed and invited in to assist them in overcoming their "double-bind."

This case study is real. We encountered it during one of the retreats we have previously led. Linda and I spent much private time with this couple, helping them open up and feel safe enough to broach the avoided issue and aid each one in communicating their emotions, thoughts, and perspective on the matter. Just opening up the discussion in a respectful and honorable way released much of the tension and struggle of their relationship. We didn't try to fix everything at once. Instead, we focused on what could be agreed on: their financial condition could no longer sustain the additional monthly payment. Everyone agreed change was necessary on the part of their parents and that the parents would either return to paying the monthly mortgage, or agree to sell the property and move to a new, affordable place. This couple recognized they did not have an immediate solution but acknowledged that God did. And based upon their agreement, they were willing to communicate with their parents, expressing to them their dilemma. This would bring everyone into the process of coming to a solution. We ended our time in prayer and asked God to provide His solution. On Monday, the day after the retreat ended, we received a phone call from the wife with an amazing story. On Sunday night, the husband's parents had called and initiated discussion regarding the dilemma. Not only were they aware and understood the financial strain they had put upon their son, but they had concluded that they would not allow the situation to continue! Of their own volition, his parents were very willing to consider selling the condo, purchase their own place, thereby, releasing them from the financial obligation. It was obvious God had orchestrated this solution and was just waiting for the couple to release their unforgiveness and open up dialogue in the Spirit, in order to come to a resolution. Wow … a truly remarkable work of God!

This was a true story with a very complicated problem, resulting in a solution only God could orchestrate. And yet, despite what your issues or conflicts are, God has the solution for each and every one of them as well! The Father cares for your issues, your concerns, your conflicts, and especially the hearts involved. Will you begin the process of allowing yourself to open up a dialogue with the Spirit, and allow Him to work things out in your life as well?

CHAPTER 7
SELFISHNESS IN CONFLICT

It should not surprise us that unbelievers are selfish by nature; and thus, act in a selfish way which promotes hurts and wounds. However, we must also accept that believers can also be very selfish people. This also, unfortunately, should not surprise us or cause us to ignore the effect of selfishness – namely that selfish people, even when they are believers, promote unforgiveness.

Have you ever been in a situation where conflict arose, and both parties involved (whether they were believers or not) acted so selfishly that they somehow ended up promoting unforgiveness? Such actions only result in deepening the level of response of all people involved. Why is that?

> *"What is the source of quarrels and conflicts among you? Is not the source your pleasures that wage war in your members? You lust and do not have; so you commit murder. You are envious and cannot obtain; so you fight and quarrel. You do not have because you do not ask. You ask and do not receive, because you ask with wrong motives, so that you may spend it on your pleasures. You adulteresses, do you not know that friendship with the world is hostility toward God? Therefore whoever wishes to be a friend of the world makes himself an enemy of God. Or do you think that the Scripture speaks to no purpose: 'He jealously desires the Spirit*

which He has made to dwell in us'? But He gives a greater grace. Therefore it says, 'God is opposed to the proud, but gives grace to the humble'... Do not speak against one another, brethren. He, who speaks against a brother or judges his brother, speaks against the law and judges the law; but if you judge the law, you are not a doer of the law but a judge of it. There is only one Lawgiver and Judge, the One who is able to save and to destroy; but who are you who judge your neighbor?" James 4: 1-6, 11-12

We all go through quarrels and disputes. But the instances where hurt and anger are maintained and not released usually result from selfish ambitions to achieve what we want, rather than being actually opposed by something or someone else. These wrong motives define so much of our problems in life. Selfishness is why we fight and quarrel, why we maintain our anger, and why we will work so hard to withhold forgiveness. All of these actions serve our own selfish purposes. And since most people, including many believers, walk daily in the flesh and self-centeredness, we should not be surprised in the least to witness such strained relationships and hardness of heart surrounding us. No one can put others in front of themselves or see their brother as more important than themselves, if they operate within the flesh, stay within partial or complete unforgiveness, and/or maintain their anger and hostility. Within disputes each person comes into the argument with their own selfish desires saying things like, "I want...," "I could really care less about what you want...," and "and I am going to do whatever I need to..." No one has successfully met expectations, and the other person becomes merely a roadblock to what we want in life or what we want them to do for us. The conflict results in both parties reiterating how they are "hurt," "angry," "haven't been heard," and so forth and so on. As a result, the wound deepens even more. However, it does not stop there. Within this selfishness, there are underlying contributors to unforgiveness, which tend to deepen the level at which we operate:

Normal:

- **Difference in personality.** God made us with a great variety of personalities, and we are naturally attracted to others with differing personalities that complement our own. However, as we get closer to and more intimate with these people to whom we were initially attracted, we find that those personality differences become irritating. For example, I am naturally aggressive and a risk taker. Linda, my spouse, is naturally verbal and risk-avoidant. We had an opportunity to invest in a new venture, which to me looked good. Because of my personality, I was willing to take the risk and wasn't worried whether or not it would work out. Linda, on the other hand, being risk averse, did not want to make the investment. Just due to our personality differences, we found ourselves in conflict. It wasn't due to any real difference of opinion – just our normal difference in personality. Before we understood this natural difference, we would battle and argue just because we disagreed. The disagreement accentuated our personality differences, naturally making things more difficult. If you were to take out all other stimuli and factors, we should know that we will continually be prone to conflict, simply due to the differences in our personalities! If we do not choose to walk in the Spirit, natural personality differences can deepen any level of unforgiveness if left unchecked.

- **Differences of opinion about how to live life.** We all come from different backgrounds, all of which shape how we live life. We have all learned differing ways to approach everyday issues. Since we were raised with different viewpoints on how to spend money, roles within marriage, how to raise children, etc., they can become stress points of natural conflict. Just because your friend or spouse or your boss or co-worker have completely different views –regarding career goals, how to spend the holidays, or what to do with relatives – it doesn't mean that they are wrong. Their views are simply different. This is often seen in political discussions. Linda and I had a retreat in Europe where the discussion drifted to political parties and how Christians could be on such different sides of the political spectrum. Linda and I had already worked through our understanding that people have different views of life, and therefore, it was not worth debating these different views (it's okay to discuss what we think, but not to arrive at arguing, debating, or hard feelings). Others, having not worked through this, experienced those harsh feelings, which inevitably arose; and consequently, so did levels of unforgiveness. We helped them work through and release those feelings, to understand that different views of life are normal and should not contribute to conflict and anger. However, being aware of these differences serve as a warning when having to come to an agreement on an issue. Be mindful that these are natural conflict areas. However, since these differences are normal and should be expected, walking in the Spirit will help to avoid deepening any level of unforgiveness.

Abnormal: These are contributing factors that are not caused by normal differences we all encounter, but rather are things caused by our selfish nature. They might be considered a normal part of life (we experience them often in our world); but they are not part of God's intended plan of how He wants life to be lived. In these situations, we wind up in an "oppressive state," causing us to carry around continual anger. Then when something happens to cause hurt or frustration, we over react, our anger deepens, and our oppression gets heavier. Some of these are as follows:

- **Continuing unmet expectations.** Disappointment and resignation can quickly lead to unforgiveness, when our expectations about what we thought life was going to be are not met.

- **Guilt.** When you cannot get over the things you have done in the past, it leads us to withhold forgiveness, especially towards ourselves.

- **Purposeful hurt.** This is when the offending person knows what you want or are striving for and purposefully opposes and comes against it. This could be done either directly or passive-aggressively.

- **Lack of follow through.** This is when someone said they would do something for you but did not keep their promise.

- **Wounds.** These are deep patterns of behavior from the past, which when the buttons are pushed, cause unhealthy responses.

At one of our retreats, we had a couple that had experienced life with all of these abnormal stressors operating at once. They had not been able to find enjoyable careers and were bouncing from job to job. As a result, they had gone into credit card debt and were under a heavy financial burden. Their life together had been a whirlwind of continuing unmet expectations, and they had developed a rather negative view of life. This type of Negativity usually reflects a low view of God and can actually reflect a deep anger and unforgiveness of God. They did not expect good things to happen to them and could not even imagine or dream of such. Furthermore, they had stopped attending church and spending time in God's word, so they carried a level of guilt knowing their life was not pleasing to God. The truth was they were mad at God, and they didn't want to spend any time with Him; but because they were believers, they carried guilt about not wanting to spend time with their Father. To complicate matters further, one of the couple's bosses was particularly harsh and power mad and would continually do things to purposely hurt and oppress his employee. Even though they were rightfully frustrated and angry at their boss, it only intensified their negative view of life. Adding insult to injury, one of their projects achieved a key milestone and even though they were promised a bonus, the company did not honor their commitment. This became a further sore spot of anger toward their boss and the company paired with deep childhood wounds of parental disappointments. All of this together created an atmosphere of guilt, lack of follow through, and an expectation of being inevitably let down. When they finally understood that the unforgiveness they carried from all these things was also reflected in the oppression they felt in their everyday life, they agreed to learn to abide in the word and experience the release of unforgiveness and the freshness of the new life. It was not a single event or an automatic transformation, but a day-by-day, month-by-month process. Through this process, God changed them internally and then changed circumstances externally to fulfill all that he wanted to do in their life. Truly, this is another remarkable example of God's power.

Though we have covered the "normal" and "abnormal" factors which contribute to how we respond to wounds, there is yet another: spiritual attack. Spiritual attacks stand uniquely different. They are normal because the enemy is alive, well, and wants to make us live apart from the spirit. Spiritual attacks are abnormal because they do not operate in what we typically experience with our five senses. Spiritual attacks, being very different by nature, also require a different approach in how to withstand them. We must recall that we are fighting against powers and principalities and not flesh and blood, and then we must understand many of the things that happen in life are direct spiritual attacks from the enemy. The goal of these attacks is to move us to a place of unforgiveness, and thus, bondage and oppression.

LIFE IN FORGIVENESS

"Put on the full armor of God, so that you will be able to stand firm against the schemes of the devil. For our struggle is not against flesh and blood, but against the rulers, against the powers, against the world forces of this darkness, against the spiritual forces of wickedness in the heavenly places." Ephesians 6: 11-12

There are schemes and strategies of the devil. The enemy is alive and very real. The enemy has strategies and schemes designed to directly affect you. The enemy's goal is to steal, kill, and destroy. This includes your heart. He will do anything he can in order to deepen your anger, hurt others, and get you to exact your own revenge by doing any or all of the following:

- Push those buttons which intensify wounds of the past
- Escalate raw feelings
- Miscommunications
- Misinterpretations
- Pile on stress and negative circumstances
- Cause distractions so people are not able to resolve issues and the wounds deepen by default

Because we're such poor communicators (usually because we don't have or don't take the time), the enemy's schemes are rather easy to carry out. At one of our retreats, a wife commented that she was tired. The husband heard that she was "sick and tired" and interpreted that to mean she was angry at him for not taking care of their finances. He then became defensive and attempted to rationalize what he was doing financially for the family. She became angry because he disre-

SELFISHNESS IN CONFLICT

garded her weariness and physical exhaustion. Their issue escalated into deeper arguing and debating - all because they didn't "hear" the same words spoken, i.e., miscommunication happened. As we helped this couple unpack their miscommunication, many factors came to light. We all discovered that the husband lived in fear when it came to his finances and projected this fear and anxiety onto his wife. His wife? Well, she was just weary from taking care of two small children without respite and missed the ability to spend time alone as a couple. Through careful communication, we were able to counteract the work of the enemy who would have taken the simple miscommunication even further into deeper levels of unforgiveness in anger. We all realized then, as we do now, how clever the enemy is and how important it is to continually process what we hear from each other so we do not give any ground to the enemy.

Take an honest assessment of your wounds, your scars, and all of your unchecked anger. Were there examples in your past, or even right now, where personality differences contributed to an otherwise simple difference of opinion? Was guilt a player in how you snapped at your spouse last week? Are your expectations of your child's education unhealthy because of your wounded past? Did the enemy twist a rather basic miscommunication into something worse, and it then became an attack? Try to assess the wounds which are the most pressing on your heart right now, and sincerely ask the Father to reveal to you what else may have contributed to the conflict other than the words said. Then be willing to receive the truth He will reveal to you, as you continue in your journey towards the freedom found in forgiveness.

CHAPTER 8
WHY WE WITHHOLD FORGIVENESS

When you take into account everything said thus far and reflect upon the words and meaning, why do we continue to hold on to unforgiveness? Why is it so difficult to move beyond the hurt and merely forgive? Why do we choose to punish ourselves by retaining our anger and animosity and keeping our hearts imprisoned, when Christ came to set us free? Reread the following passage:

> *"For this reason God gave them over to degrading passions; for their women exchanged the natural function for that which is unnatural, and in the same way also the men abandoned the natural function of the woman and burned in their desire toward one another, men with men committing indecent acts and receiving in their own persons the due penalty of their error. And just as they did not see fit to acknowledge God any longer, God gave them over to a depraved mind, to do those things which are not proper, being filled with all unrighteousness, wickedness, greed, evil; full of envy, murder, strife, deceit, malice; they are gossips, slanderers, haters of God, insolent, arrogant, boastful, inventors of evil, disobedient to parents, without understanding, untrustworthy, unloving, unmerciful; and although they know the ordinance of God, that those who practice such things are worthy of death, they not only do the same, but also give hearty approval to those who practice them." Romans 1:26–32*

WHY WE WITHHOLD FORGIVENESS

When our anger deepens, it turns into bitterness and strife. We are found without understanding, and thus, become creatures that do not love, do not show mercy, and do not forgive. Our emotions are completely unstable and are anything but neutral. Unless we are walking according to the Spirit, such fleshly actions and selfishness will only become worse, more acute and our unforgiveness will follow suit. This is why our society is the way it is. Unforgiveness is running rampant in our world and has resulted in a pandemic of wounded, broken, and bleeding individuals who show no mercy or hope. We show no hope, because we have failed to receive hope from the Giver of Life when we choose to hold on to our own ways and refuse to forgive. Even believers, who have been so beautifully forgiven, refuse to forgive others because they do not walk in God's Spirit and in His love. People are in pain, real pain, and many times such pain and deep wounds are too deep to reach without forgiveness. You see, with forgiveness true healing can be experienced, and without it our wounds continue to rot and the disease of Self clutches all the more firmly. We are so wounded and have been for so long that we have retrained our minds to shy away from any type of constructive criticism. The lessons we have learned along the way have taught us that quite clearly. "It is much easier to avoid conflict altogether and sweep it under the rug than to fully resolve the issues," we chant over and over in our minds, we eventually believe the lie. We tell ourselves that even if we did try to resolve any conflict, we would be outmaneuvered, or it would just turn into another fight, so why even try? The danger of this thinking is that these patterns eventually cement themselves into your brain and become your new norm, meaning the normal way you live your life and handle any and all current and future conflict. You resign to the fact that you must simply, "live with it." Hope of believing there is anything better slowly dies.

Yet, the most prevalent reason we withhold forgiveness is: **WE CONFUSE FORGIVENESS WITH RECONCILIATION**. Most people tend to believe one or all of the following statements.

If I forgive, then I:

- Will never be able to share my real feelings, hurts, pain and anger

- May stimulate further conflict with the other person, who may be stronger than me, and it will just make things worse. This strength may be in personality, emotion, hostility, or in authority over me (i.e., a mother or father even though I am an adult), so I just resign to the fact it is just too much trouble

- Will reinforce that the actions done to me were actually okay and my offender will never have to deal with or suffer any consequences for what they did. I fear or believe they will only become stronger in their selfishness

- Only end up sanctioning, promoting, and allowing the harming person to do these actions to me over and over again in the future

We have convinced ourselves that by holding onto unforgiveness, we control the dynamics. We make sure these things (see above) do

WHY WE WITHHOLD FORGIVENESS

not happen. In fact, by maintaining coldness and distance through unforgiveness, we think we can:

- Protect our heart from further hurts and pains
- Make a statement that what the other person did was wrong and they should feel-
  - Guilt
  - Suffer the consequences of not having me serve them and miss out on the benefits of the past relationship
  - My disapproval
  - Sad at our changed relationship
  - Not allow the other person to do this again easily and keep hurting us. Such actions deaden our pain and allow the wounds to scab.
  - Make it easier to function by avoiding conflict altogether and setting up walls around us for protection.

As is often the case, our perception of reality is not actually real. In fact, what really happens to the heart is quite opposite:

"Watch over your heart with all diligence, for from it flows the springs of life." Proverbs 4:23

"The fool has said in his heart, 'There is no God.' They are corrupt, they have committed abominable deeds; There is no one who does good." Psalm 14:1

"Why do You stand afar off, O Lord? Why do You hide Yourself

in times of trouble? In pride the wicked hotly pursue the afflicted; Let them be caught in the plots which they have devised. For the wicked boasts of his heart's desire, and the greedy man curses and spurns the Lord. The wicked, in the haughtiness of his countenance, does not seek Him. All his thoughts are, 'There is no God.'" Psalm 10:1-4

"Thus says the Lord, 'Cursed is the man who trusts in mankind and makes flesh his strength, and whose heart turns away from the Lord. For he will be like a bush in the desert and will not see when prosperity comes, but will live in stony wastes in the wilderness, a land of salt without inhabitant…The heart is more deceitful than all else and is desperately sick; Who can understand it?'" Jeremiah 17:5-6, 9

Up to this point, we may have tried to convince ourselves that withholding forgiveness to those who have wounded us actually protects us, but that is a lie. God's Word says as we continually walk in the flesh and operate in the carnal self, we experience the three consequences listed in Romans 8:5-8: death of the spirit, enmity against God, and the inability to please God. It's as if we operate like there was no God, and believers operate as practical atheists. Our hearts subsequently move deeper into unforgiveness, and we have little control over the emotions we experience. These emotions include:

- Deepening of Wounds
- Roots of bitterness
- Edginess

WHY WE WITHHOLD FORGIVENESS

- Frustration
- Low grade anger
- Short fuses, triggers and hot buttons
- Bondage and being guarded
- Negative energy, negative outlook, and being critical

Unforgiveness is literally the root of Christians living in bondage, oppression, and unhappiness instead of the fullness of all Christ promised. Our world is becoming more and more stressful, and we are bombarded by selfishness and messages that looking out for self the only way to get what you deserve. And if we don't go after what is rightfully ours, we will be doormats and open for continual abuse. We have accepted that living in unforgiveness is normal. Because of the dysfunctions of our families, our work, our friendships – and even our church communities - we are continually wounded and hurt, plus angry with roots of bitterness. While it seems difficult to even think that we can reach a modest level of forgiveness toward those who have hurt us, we mostly hold on to unforgiveness because of our misunderstanding about reconciliation. We actually use it as a tool to establish a wall that we think is protecting our hearts and souls and the circumstances of our life. What we don't understand is that it is causing us great pain, including physical problems, mental and spiritual difficulties, as well as the inability to enjoy the abundant life promised to us by our Lord Jesus. As we gain this understanding, let us pursue God's truth that can free us from this awful situation.

Look at your life and your attitude towards life as a whole. How would you define it? Do you experience joy, peace, and general order? Do you generally live in fear and are critical of others? Does your life reflect the promises of Scripture for those who walk in the Spirit, or does it look quite the opposite? Be honest with yourself, because the fruit of living in the Spirit cannot be falsely generated. If you are not enjoying the abundant life Christ promised to His children, then begin to look at unforgiveness in your life. Against whom do you hold grudges or hostility? Who are you icy towards, or at whom do you roll your eyes when they walk into the room? Start with the obvious ones, and then allow the Spirit to guide you into further truth as you begin to look at forgiving that high school teacher, the college roommate, your uncle, or your boss.

CHAPTER 9
DEFINING FORGIVENESS

Before we jump right into defining what forgiveness is, I want to give a very practical example from my own life. Do you remember a few chapters ago when I was discussing my relationship with my mother? It was through that strained relationship that God revealed to us my bondage and oppression contained within unforgiveness. However, it was also through this process and the scriptures we studied addressing forgiveness that we remembered another situation where we experienced and were shown forgiveness.

In college, I worked for an advertising company and was responsible for compiling all materials needed for use in client presentations, (remember, these were the days before computers, so all the materials were hard copy). Being bright and continually demonstrating competence in completing projects, the partners began trusting my ability to correctly execute given assignments. During one week in particular, I received an assignment requiring a very lengthy and complex list of materials to be compiled for an important meeting hoping to secure a new client. The presentation package was put together, and I treated it like the rest of my projects at the time and believed it had been done correctly. The day before the presentation, one of the partners called and asked me to verify that all of the information was correct and to confirm with him when I had finished checking. I said I would call him back. However, the next day I had a term paper due and needed to stay up late to complete it. Since I assumed the packet was correct, I did not take the extra time to physically double check my work. Yet, I called the partner anyway and told him everything was in order. The next day during the presentation, the final three slides, the "punch line" of the entire meeting, were missing. Not only were the partners not able to illustrate their creative approach to their client, they also presented themselves as an agency not focused on details. Needless to say, my company lost that account and the fault rested squarely upon my shoulders. I failed to fulfill my assignment in addition to lying about verifying my work. I had every right to be fired. Yet, I was shown forgiveness and grace. When one of the partners called me into his office, he discussed how my lack of integrity affected him, his business integrity, as well as the integrity of the agency. Then he said he was giving me a gift in keeping my job and that he believed I would learn a valuable life lesson as a result of this mistake. He encouraged me to leave my mistake behind me and only look forward to becoming the best I could be. Instead of firing me, he gave me even more responsibility! What an amazing example of forgiveness, and what a wonderful demonstration of what forgiveness really looks like.

In light of this story from my past, I ask you: What exactly is forgiveness? What are the true dimensions of forgiveness? What does it feel like? We can start to explain forgiveness by saying it includes having compassionate feelings towards a person who wronged you, and these feelings allow you to pardon them. But forgiveness is more than mere feelings. When you forgive, you are releasing your anger against your offender and have decided to terminate all resentment towards them. So all of that indignation and anger, which bubbled up as the result of a difference of opinions or a simple mistake or offense, no longer remains held against your wrongdoer. You decide to let it go; you choose not to hold on to the offense any longer. Remember the agency partner? He addressed my mistakes, which were worthy of being fired, and told me to learn from them. Not only that, but he chose to not hold those against me and encouraged me to not hold them against myself – to move on and simply use my mistakes as a springboard for becoming even better. Those feelings of compassion, which allowed him to forgive me and that allow you to so forgive others, come from God himself. In fact, God's very nature is the compassion and grace He freely bestows upon us. We are the ones who deserve the wrath and anger of God because of the sin we have committed, but God releases that wrath and no longer holds it against us. God forgives us, and simply, lets our sin go.

"If You, Lord, should mark iniquities, O Lord, who could stand? But there is forgiveness with You, that You may be feared... O Israel, hope in the Lord; For with the Lord there is loving-kindness, and with Him is abundant redemption." Psalm 130:3-4, 7

"The Lord is compassionate and gracious, slow to anger and abounding in loving-kindness. He will not always strive with us, nor will He keep His anger forever. He has not dealt with us according to our sins, nor rewarded us according to our iniquities. For as high as the heavens are above the earth, so great is His loving-kindness toward those who fear Him. As far as the east is

from the west, so far has He removed our transgressions from us."
Psalm 103:8-12

"To the Lord our God belong compassion and forgiveness, for we have rebelled against Him" Daniel 9:9

Again, God's nature is to forgive. He is wholly different than humanity in that forgiveness is not something he chooses to do; rather, it is who He is. God cannot help but forgive, because the Great I AM is the one who forgives. Without this forgiveness from a holy God, we would have no chance of a relationship with Him. The very same God who created the universe with only a breath cares deeply for us. Yes, we deserve wrath and ultimate separation from the Lord, but God offers us an incredible gift. We are always being offered an intimate relationship with Him and to constantly walk with Him in the Spirit. This gift of intimacy with the Almighty is available, only because forgiveness from the same God is possible and freely offered. But God's nature does not only include forgiveness; His broader nature includes much more.

God is Eternally Holy or Perfectly Righteous

"And one called out to another and said, 'Holy, Holy, Holy, is the Lord of hosts, the whole earth is full of His glory.'" Isaiah 6:3

And the four living creatures, each one of them having six wings, are full of eyes around and within; and day and night they do not cease to say, 'Holy, holy, holy is the Lord God, the Almighty, who was and who is and who is to come'... 'Worthy are You, our Lord and our God, to receive glory and honor and power; for You created all things, and because of Your will they existed, and were created.'" Revelation 4:8,11

When Scripture speaks of Holiness, it means something or someone who is wholly distinct, separate, and in a class all by themselves. R. C. Sproul explains it this way in his book The Holiness of God:

"The primary meaning of holy is 'separate.' It comes from an ancient word that meant, 'to cut,' or 'to separate.' Perhaps even more accurate would be the phrase 'a cut above something.' When we find a garment or another piece of merchandise that is outstanding, that has a superior excellence, we use the expression that it is 'a cut above the rest.'" [1]

So, God is unique and has no rivals or competition. He is completely different than anyone or anything else in all creation. But God's holiness encompasses so much more. God's holiness also means He is worthy of all honor, power, and glory (praise, fame, and/or adoration). If God is worth such accolades, which we call worship, He must also be pure, having no wrong or evil in Him – which is true! God is good; He is morally pure; He loves perfectly and is perfect love, and every action He does is the same. God is the only perfect being, and He is perfectly righteous (morally upright and above reproach) to forgive others, as He has forgiven us.

Take a minute to let all these wonderful truths sink into your head and heart. The last thing you need to do is to rush over the truths contained within these scriptures. Ask yourself, what does it mean to me that God's very nature is to forgive? How does this one statement change your perception of God and your relationship with Him? When you begin to grasp this reality, it makes more sense to also embrace how God is truly other, wholly different than the humanity He created. Only the One who is wholly different, who is Holy, can have a nature defined by forgiveness. This forgiveness, spurred on by His never-ending love towards His children, is waiting for you to receive it. Spend ample time letting these statements become truth to you, life for you, and thank the Father for His nature.

CHAPTER 10
GOD'S ORIGINAL PLAN

This holy, wholly other, and different God delighted in creating, and He still does! So, when God created Adam and Eve in the garden, He created them perfectly. They were holy as He is holy, perfect and righteous. He created them to have an exceptional life and constant communion with Himself. God created man to have a full and enjoyable relationship with their creator.

> "Then God said, 'Let Us make man in Our image, according to Our likeness; and let them rule over the fish of the sea and over the birds of the sky and over the cattle and over all the earth, and over every creeping thing that creeps on the earth.' God created man in His own image, in the image of God He created him; male and female He created them. God blessed them; and God said to them, 'Be fruitful and multiply, and fill the earth, and subdue it; and rule over the fish of the sea and over the birds of the sky and over every living thing that moves on the earth.' Then God said, 'Behold, I have given you every plant yielding seed that is on the surface of all the earth, and every tree which has fruit yielding seed; it shall be food for you; and to every beast of the earth and to every bird of the sky and to everything that moves on the earth which has life, I have given every green plant for food; and it was so. God saw all that He had made, and

behold, it was very good. And there was evening and there was morning, the sixth day. Thus the heavens and the earth were completed, and all their hosts. By the seventh day God completed His work which He had done, and He rested on the seventh day from all His work which He had done. Then God blessed the seventh day and sanctified it, because in it He rested from all His work which God had created and made.

"This is the account of the heavens and the earth when they were created, in the day that the Lord God made earth and heaven. Now no shrub of the field was yet in the earth, and no plant of the field had yet sprouted, for the Lord God had not sent rain upon the earth, and there was no man to cultivate the ground. But a mist used to rise from the earth and water the whole surface of the ground. Then the Lord God formed man of dust from the ground, and breathed into his nostrils the breath of life; and man became a living being. The Lord God planted a garden toward the east, in Eden; and there He placed the man whom He had formed. Out of the ground the Lord God caused to grow every tree that is pleasing to the sight and good for food; the tree of life also in the midst of the garden, and the tree of the knowledge of good and evil. Now a river flowed out of Eden to water the garden; and from there it divided and became four rivers. The name of the first is Pishon; it flows around the whole land of Havilah, where there is gold. The gold of that land is good; the bdellium and the onyx stone are there. The name of the second river is Gihon; it flows around the whole land of Cush.

GOD'S ORIGINAL PLAN

The name of the third river is Tigris; it flows east of Assyria. And the fourth river is the Euphrates. Then the Lord God took the man and put him into the Garden of Eden to cultivate it and keep it. The Lord God commanded the man, saying, 'From any tree of the garden you may eat freely; but from the tree of the knowledge of good and evil you shall not eat, for in the day that you eat from it you will surely die.' Then the Lord God said, 'It is not good for the man to be alone; I will make him a helper suitable for him.' Out of the ground the Lord God formed every beast of the field and every bird of the sky, and brought them to the man to see what he would call them; and whatever the man called a living creature, that was its name. The man gave names to all the cattle, and to the birds of the sky, and to every beast of the field, but for Adam there was not found a helper suitable for him. So the Lord God caused a deep sleep to fall upon the man, and he slept; then He took one of his ribs and closed up the flesh at that place. The Lord God fashioned into a woman the rib which He had taken from the man, and brought her to the man. The man said, 'This is now bone of my bones, and flesh of my flesh; She shall be called Woman, because she was taken out of Man.' For this reason a man shall leave his father and his mother, and be joined to his wife; and they shall become one flesh. And the man and his wife were both naked and were not ashamed." Genesis 1:26 – 2:25

God's original plan and intention for His most beloved creation, man and woman, was for them to live in perpetual beauty – on the earth. Upon this earth was everything needed for them to not merely exist, but to flourish amidst its beauty. When God creates something, He indeed shows off his power and creativity. God wanted mankind to have exceptional life. **This exceptional life included extraordinary authority.** Adam and Eve were charged by God to control the earth and to rule over all the animals. They were to do so in a caring manner, which would lead to greater flocks and herds, as well as cultivating more abundant and fruitful trees and other growing plants. This was also remarkable work to do. God was entrusting Adam and Eve with the rest of His creation! That is quite a charge placed upon them. **They were to experience exceptional work** - not tedious or laborious. In the beginning, work was good and profitable and even enjoyable.

Not only were they created to have amazing authority and work, but within that authority and work, **they were provided exceptional provision**. Everything they could possibly want or need was laid before them in Eden. There was an abundance of ripe and juicy fruit, vegetables, nuts, and roots for them to feast upon each and every day. God not only gave them enough to survive, but He provided Adam and Eve more than they would ever need. God gave Adam and Eve the **charge together to enjoy an exceptional marriage**. They were married to one another so therefore had the shared responsibility of tending God's entire creation. God not only presented a helpmate suitable for Adam at the appropriate time, but He did so from a bone intended to guard Adam's heart. This is quite a picture. Woman's original purpose was to become such a helper to her husband that she not only helped guard his heart, but she would be indispensable in his life – to always be at his side, wherever he went. Adam and Eve were two people operating as one flesh: in agreement on purpose, direction, intention, and with their hearts in their hands. This was an exceptional marriage. There was no shame, no guilt, and no past to worry about on either side. They were free to find pleasure in each other and in each other's company with no jealousy or divided attentions. They were free to enjoy their relationship with all of creation and **relish the exceptional identity** they had been given. What was this unique and remarkable identity? They were God's pet project: the only creation made by God's hands, given the breath of God, and the only one made in His image. They were image bearers of the creator and walked among the rest of creation as the representation of God. Everything Adam did reflected the will and desire of his creator, but it was always under the authority of God Almighty. Adam and Eve each had the unique ability and identity to represent God in both His nature and His desired task upon the Earth.

And how did they know so clearly God's design for them within all of creation? That has everything to do with their extraordinary relationship with the creator of the heavens and earth. There was absolutely nothing in the beginning which would hinder the **exceptional communion** experienced between creator and creation. Later in Genesis, scripture states how God walked in the cool of the day with Adam. God walked with them! When you or I walk with someone on a consistent basis, we rarely do so in silence. Some of the best conversations can be experienced while walking with another, because in those moments you are sharing life while sharing strides. Laughing becomes commonplace as you may reminisce of past memories or jokes, and dreaming the big dreams seems nearly attainable when you have a friend by your side, encouraging you along the path. God had an intimate relationship with his beloved man and woman, fully intending that such a relationship would be available and desired by all forthcoming generations. It was in these early days that Adam and Eve naturally walked each day guided by the Spirit, because the very Spirit of God was resident with them. All three parts of their humanity: the flesh (material), the soul (the seat of the personality, will, intellect and emotions), and the Spirit were all of one accord. Unfortunately, things did not stay in such beautiful harmony for long.

Such beauty and such harmony can make one's soul ache for that which has been lost. Our spirits know that we have lost that which our Heavenly Father did originally intended for us, but this is not the time to dwell on past failures. It is the time to be thankful for God's original intention for us! His intentions for us remain the same, even though we were not created as Adam and Eve. Dream for a bit. What would your life look like if this very same authority, provision, enjoyable work, marriage, and identity were offered to you right now? What if you had them right now? Let your soul dare to dream this God-sized dream and become like a child once again … daydream about riding on elephants, about grapes the size of a fist, or swimming with sharks without fear. Whatever it is, fantasize about God's original intentions and start hoping for the future!

CHAPTER 11
OUR FAILING AND FALLING

When God created the garden and the first humans in perfection, He told Adam and Eve they could eat of any tree except for the tree of the knowledge of good and evil. Remember, Eden is said to have had four rivers coming together in it. Although the exact size of Eden is unsure, we can assume it was quite expansive. This being said, there was a plethora of fruit bearing trees from which man and woman could eat, and only one tree to avoid. Even with myriads of choices for food, Adam and Even chose to eat of that tree, against the will of God; and because of their willful act of the flesh, they sinned. This changed everything.

> *"Now the serpent was more crafty than any beast of the field which the Lord God had made. And he said to the woman, 'Indeed, has God said, "You shall not eat from any tree of the garden"?' The woman said to the serpent, 'From the fruit of the trees of the garden we may eat; but from the fruit of the tree which is in the middle of the garden, God has said, "You shall not eat from it or touch it, or you will die."' The serpent said to the woman, 'You surely will not die! For God knows that in the day you eat from it your eyes will be opened, and you will be like God, knowing good and evil.' When the woman saw that the tree was good for food, and that it was a delight to the eyes, and that*

the tree was desirable to make one wise, she took from its fruit and ate; and she gave also to her husband with her, and he ate. Then the eyes of both of them were opened, and they knew that they were naked; and they sewed fig leaves together and made themselves loin coverings. They heard the sound of the Lord God walking in the garden in the cool of the day, and the man and his wife hid themselves from the presence of the Lord God among the trees of the garden. Then the Lord God called to the man, and said to him, 'Where are you?' He said, 'I heard the sound of You in the garden, and I was afraid because I was naked; so I hid myself.' And He said, 'Who told you that you were naked? Have you eaten from the tree of which I commanded you not to eat?' The man said, 'The woman whom You gave to be with me, she gave me from the tree, and I ate.' Then the Lord God said to the woman, 'What is this you have done?' And the woman said, 'The serpent deceived me, and I ate.' The Lord God said to the serpent, 'Because you have done this, cursed are you more than all cattle, and more than every beast of the field; On your belly you will go, and dust you will eat all the days of your life; And I will put enmity between you and the woman, and between your seed and her seed; He shall bruise you on the head, and you shall bruise him on the heel.' To the woman He said, 'I will greatly multiply your pain in childbirth, in pain you will bring forth children; yet your desire will be for your husband, and he will rule over you.' Then to Adam He said, 'Because you have listened to the voice of your wife, and have eaten from the tree

OUR FAILING AND FALLING

about which I commanded you, saying, "You shall not eat from it"; Cursed is the ground because of you; in toil you will eat of it all the days of your life. Both thorns and thistles it shall grow for you; and you will eat the plants of the field; by the sweat of your face you will eat bread, till you return to the ground, because from it you were taken; for you are dust, and to dust you shall return.' Now the man called his wife's name Eve, because she was the mother of all the living. The Lord God made garments of skin for Adam and his wife, and clothed them. Then the Lord God said, 'Behold, the man has become like one of Us, knowing good and evil; and now, he might stretch out his hand, and take also from the tree of life, and eat, and live forever' — therefore the Lord God sent him out from the garden of Eden, to cultivate the ground from which he was taken. So He drove the man out; and at the east of the garden of Eden He stationed the cherubim and the flaming sword which turned every direction to guard the way to the tree of life." Genesis 3:1-24

Yes, Adam and Eve were deceived and tempted by the serpent, and no, they could not have prevented the temptation from happening. However, they still chose to go against God's command regarding the fruit. This decision, this disobedience caused them to perish. This act caused their spirits to literally die. That wonderful Spirit-given holiness and perfect righteousness originally imparted by God was now gone forever. The sweet communion they had previously shared with God was also severed, and they found themselves forever separated from a Holy God. Sin had killed their spirit and allowed physical death to creep in as well. Because of their sin and exercise of self-will, they fully deserved God's eternal wrath and anger. The creation had deeply wronged the holy creator, but we know the story does not end there. Hope still exists.

> *"If You, Lord, should mark iniquities, O Lord, who could stand?"* Psalm 130:3

> *"For all have sinned and fall short of the glory of God."* Romans 3:23

> *"And do not enter into judgment with Your servant, for in Your sight no man living is righteous."* Psalm 143:2

> *"He will not always strive with us, nor will He keep His anger forever. He has not dealt with us according to our sins, nor rewarded us according to our iniquities."* Psalm 103:9-10

Since God's very nature is forgiveness, He did not eternally separate Himself from His creation by demanding us to achieve perfection and holiness on our own. God knew we could not achieve such a demand. He knew this inability on our part would result in eternal separation. So, He gave Moses the law. In the law, the issue of sin was addressed through the sacrificing of a perfect lamb by the High Priest. This was done every year on the Day of Atonement. Through the shedding of innocent blood, through the killing of an innocent lamb's life, the sin of Israel was atoned for, or satisfied, repaired, and reconciled (Leviticus 16-17). But the essence of the law was ultimately to remind mankind they cannot remedy their sin by themselves. The

OUR FAILING AND FALLING

lamb's sacrifice was a foreshadowing of the last Lamb to be killed for humanity.

Many of us are overly familiar with the story of the Garden of Eden and the snake, the fruit, etc. In our over-familiarity with this story, we can sometimes become immune to the gravity of sin in history and sin in our own lives. Make no mistake, sin and eternal separation from God is real and is painful to the heart of our Father. His nature is to forgive, but because He is holy, He cannot allow imperfection into His presence. This proves a problem. How can a holy God reconcile Himself to imperfect humanity? Forgiveness … but this goes way beyond following a set of laws and way beyond doing our "best." It has everything to do with a Lamb. If you have never acknowledged your sinfulness to God, do it now. Accept the fact you aren't perfect and are in good company for not being perfect! Remember, none of us are. However, there is hope beyond measure in knowing God understands and is fully aware of our inability to achieve perfection on our own … which is why He made a way.

CHAPTER 12
LOVE'S VICTORY

So what is this way that was made? What is the hope amidst a seemingly hopeless situation? The New Testament tells of God's perfect lamb, Jesus, "God with Us" dying on our behalf. Through God's forgiving nature, Christ exchanged His own life for ours as the remedy for reconciliation and forgave us our sin. The Father's only begotten Son and our High Priest died, sacrificed Himself, in order to fulfill the law to restore communion. He died as the propitiation (appeasement or placation) of our sin; He died as a justification of (setting us free from) sin; and His perfect righteousness and holiness is given to us in exchange. He died to take the penalty of judgment for all His creation and, in turn, offers that same creation the opportunity to be free. Jesus died once for all mankind, and the full appeasement of sin has been completed; it has been finished. Forgiveness has been fulfilled for all people, for all time.

> *"But now apart from the Law the righteousness of God has been manifested, being witnessed by the Law and the Prophets, even the righteousness of God through faith in Jesus Christ for all those who believe; for there is no distinction; for all have sinned and fall short of the glory of God, being justified as a gift by His grace through the redemption which is in Christ Jesus; whom God displayed publicly as a propitiation in His blood through faith.*

This was to demonstrate His righteousness, because in the forbearance of God He passed over the sins previously committed; for the demonstration, I say, of His righteousness at the present time, so that He would be just and the justifier of the one who has faith in Jesus." Romans 3:21-16

"In Him we have redemption through His blood, the forgiveness of our trespasses, according to the riches of His grace which He lavished on us. In all wisdom and insight He made known to us the mystery of His will, according to His kind intention which He purposed in Him with a view to an administration suitable to the fullness of the times, that is, the summing up of all things in Christ, things in the heavens and things on the earth. In Him also we have obtained an inheritance, having been predestined according to His purpose who works all things after the counsel of His will, to the end that we who were the first to hope in Christ would be to the praise of His glory." Ephesians 1:7-12

"Now even the first covenant had regulations of divine worship and the earthly sanctuary. For there was a tabernacle prepared, the outer one, in which were the lampstand and the table and the sacred bread; this is called the holy place. Behind the second veil there was a tabernacle which is called the Holy of Holies, having a golden altar of incense and the ark of the covenant covered on all sides with gold, in which was a golden jar holding the manna, and Aaron's rod which budded, and the tables of the covenant; and above it were the cherubim of glory overshadow-

ing the mercy seat; but of these things we cannot now speak in detail. Now when these things have been so prepared, the priests are continually entering the outer tabernacle performing the divine worship, but into the second, only the high priest enters once a year, not without taking blood, which he offers for himself and for the sins of the people committed in ignorance. The Holy Spirit is signifying this, that the way into the holy place has not yet been disclosed while the outer tabernacle is still standing, which is a symbol for the present time. Accordingly both gifts and sacrifices are offered which cannot make the worshiper perfect in conscience, since they relate only to food and drink and various washings, regulations for the body imposed until a time of reformation. But when Christ appeared as a high priest of the good things to come, He entered through the greater and more perfect tabernacle, not made with hands, that is to say, not of this creation; and not through the blood of goats and calves, but through His own blood, He entered the holy place once for all, having obtained eternal redemption. For if the blood of goats and bulls and the ashes of a heifer sprinkling those who have been defiled sanctify for the cleansing of the flesh, how much more will the blood of Christ, who through the eternal Spirit offered Himself without blemish to God, cleanse your conscience from dead works to serve the living God? For this reason He is the mediator of a new covenant, so that, since a death has taken place for the redemption of the transgressions that were committed under the first covenant, those who have been called may receive the *promise of the eternal inheritance. For where a covenant is, there must of necessity be the death of the one who made it. For a covenant is valid only when men are dead, for it is never in force while the one who made it lives. Therefore even the first covenant was not inaugurated without blood. For when every commandment had been spoken by Moses to all the people according to the Law, he took the blood of the calves and the goats, with water and scarlet wool and hyssop, and sprinkled both the book itself and all the people, saying, 'This is the blood of the covenant which God commanded you.' And in the same way he sprinkled both the tabernacle and all the vessels of the ministry with the blood. And according to the Law, one may almost say, all things are cleansed with blood, and without shedding of blood there is no forgiveness. Therefore it was necessary for the copies of the things in the heavens to be cleansed with these, but the heavenly things themselves with better sacrifices than these. For Christ did not enter a holy place made with hands, a mere copy of the true one, but into heaven itself, now to appear in the presence of God for us; nor was it that He would offer Himself often, as the high priest enters the holy place year by year with blood that is not his own. Otherwise, He would have needed to suffer often since the foundation of the world; but now once at the consummation of the ages He has been manifested to put away sin by the sacrifice of Himself. And inasmuch as it is appointed for men to die once and after this comes judgment, so Christ also, having been offered once to bear the sins of many, will appear a second time for salvation without reference to sin, to those who eagerly await Him. For the Law, since it has only a shadow of the good things to come and not the very form of things, can never, by the same sacrifices which they offer continually year by year, make perfect those who draw near. Otherwise, would they not have ceased to be offered, because the worshipers, having once been cleansed, would no longer have had consciousness of sins? But in those sacrifices there is a reminder of sins year by year. For it is impossible for the blood of bulls and goats to take away sins. Therefore, when He comes into the world, He says, 'Sacrifice and offering You have not desired, but a body You have prepared for Me; in whole burnt offerings and sacrifices for sin You have taken no pleasure. Then I said, "Behold, I have come (In the scroll of the book it is written of Me) To do Your will, O God."' After saying above, 'Sacrifices and offerings and whole burnt offerings and sacrifices for sin You have not desired, nor have You taken pleasure in them' (which are offered according to the Law), then He said, 'Behold, I have come to do Your will.' He takes away the first in order to establish the second. By this will, we have been sanctified through the offering of the body of Jesus Christ once for all. Every priest stands daily ministering and offering time after time the same sacrifices, which can never take away sins; but He, having offered one sacrifice for sins for all time, sat down at the right hand of God, waiting from that time onward until His enemies be made a footstool for His feet. For by one offering He has perfected for all time those who are sanctified. And the Holy*

LOVE'S VICTORY

Spirit also testifies to us; for after saying, 'This is the covenant that I will make with them after those days, says the Lord: I will put My laws upon their heart, and on their mind I will write them,' He then says, 'And their sins and their lawless deeds I will remember no more.' Now where there is forgiveness of these things, there is no longer any offering for sin." Hebrews 9:1 – 10:18

"Beloved, let us love one another, for love is from God; and everyone who loves is born of God and knows God. The one who does not love does not know God, for God is love. By this the love of God was manifested in us, that God has sent His only begotten Son into the world so that we might live through Him. In this is love, not that we loved God, but that He loved us and sent His Son to be the propitiation for our sins. Beloved, if God so loved us, we also ought to love one another." 1 John 4:7-11

"and He Himself is the propitiation for our sins; and not for ours only, but also for those of the whole world." 1 John 2:2

"so that whoever believes will in Him have eternal life. For God so loved the world, that He gave His only begotten Son, that whoever believes in Him shall not perish, but have eternal life. For God did not send the Son into the world to judge the world, but that the world might be saved through Him. He who believes in Him is not judged; he who does not believe has been judged already, because he has not believed in the name of the only begotten Son of God. This is the judgment, that the Light has come into the world, and men loved the darkness rather than the

LIFE IN FORGIVENESS

Light, for their deeds were evil. For everyone who does evil hates the Light, and does not come to the Light for fear that his deeds will be exposed. But he who practices the truth comes to the Light, so that his deeds may be manifested as having been wrought in God." John 3:15-21

Mankind was separated from God because of sin. Upon entering at the Garden of Eden, sin killed man's spirit and the intimate communion once shared between God and man and woman was irrevocably broken. Sin, evil, and a self-satisfying will have no fellowship or association with Holy God. Nevertheless, love and forgiveness prevails. God Himself provided the remedy needed to satisfy His holy demands to restore the broken relationship. God became man in Jesus, dwelt among mankind, and then died for humanity's sin. If God had to implement forgiveness based merely on when and if we deserve it, God never would have offered it. Again, forgiveness from God has nothing to do with what we deserve. It is based solely on God's nature … who He IS. God forgives. To anyone who asks, God passes over our sins, remembers them no more, and replaces our sin with a cloak of His own righteousness.

Such a difficult concept is sometimes more easily understood through fiction. If you have read Chronicles of Narnia, then you may remember the character, Aslan. He was the lion who in The Magician's Nephew sung the world of Narnia into existence – everything from the stars to the grass, Aslan sung it into existence. The story continues in The Lion, the Witch, and the Wardrobe, where the White Witch deceives Edmund, and his traitorous actions require him to die. However, the creator of Narnia, Aslan, dies in Edmund's place. This was the horrible and torturous death of a sinless one on behalf of a sinner deserving death. Such is the story of Christ in reality. A sinless one died on behalf of sinners. Again, the creator dies on behalf of the creation.

But Aslan did not remain dead. He broke the stone table and rose from the dead victorious. Likewise, neither did Jesus remain dead; otherwise, we would have no hope. In Christ's death, He took upon Himself the sin of the world and rose from the dead only a few days later. Once He satisfied God the Father's requirement for sin upon Himself, He rose from the grave victorious and was resurrected into an eternal new life, even more abundant than before. And with this resurrection, the law (what the stone table represents) was put to death. Jesus, after all, was and is the resurrection and the life.

> *"So when Jesus came, He found that he had already been in the tomb four days. Now Bethany was near Jerusalem, about two miles off; and many of the Jews had come to Martha and Mary, to console them concerning their brother. Martha therefore, when she heard that Jesus was coming, went to meet Him, but Mary stayed at the house. Martha then said to Jesus, 'Lord, if You had been here, my brother would not have died. Even now I know that whatever You ask of God, God will give You.' Jesus *said to her, 'Your brother will rise again.' Martha said to Him, 'I know that he will rise again in the resurrection on the last day.' Jesus said to her, 'I am the resurrection and the life; he who believes in Me will live even if he dies, and everyone who lives and believes*

in Me will never die. Do you believe this?' She said to Him, 'Yes, Lord; I have believed that You are the Christ, the Son of God, even He who comes into the world.'" John 11:17-27

"'If you love Me, you will keep My commandments. I will ask the Father, and He will give you another Helper, that He may be with you forever; that is the Spirit of truth, whom the world cannot receive, because it does not see Him or know Him, but you know Him because He abides with you and will be in you. I will not leave you as orphans; I will come to you. After a little while the world will no longer see Me, but you will see Me; because I live, you will live also. In that day you will know that I am in My Father, and you in Me, and I in you. He who has My commandments and keeps them is the one who loves Me; and he who loves Me will be loved by My Father, and I will love him and will disclose Myself to him.' Judas (not Iscariot) said to Him, 'Lord, what then has happened that You are going to disclose Yourself to us and not to the world?' Jesus answered and said to him, 'If anyone loves Me, he will keep My word; and My Father will love him, and We will come to him and make Our abode with him. He who does not love Me does not keep My words; and the word which you hear is not Mine, but the Father's who sent Me. These things I have spoken to you while abiding with you. But the Helper, the Holy Spirit, whom the Father will send in My name, He will teach you all things, and bring to your remembrance all that I said to you.'" John 14:15-24

LOVE'S VICTORY

"The thief comes only to steal and kill and destroy; I came that they may have life, and have it abundantly." John 10:10

It is a paradox. Through His death, He attained life. He exchanged His life for mine, for yours, and for all of mankind's. When we die to self, we live in the Spirit. Only in God's economy do equations work out like this. Everything God did through sending His Son, everything His Son, Jesus, did was due to the nature of forgiveness inherent within the Almighty. Because of this forgiveness, and only because of it, do we have the opportunity to once again be restored to our former, exceptional place in life. Our extraordinary identity can be regained, and then some. We can exercise our exceptional authority and take ground against the kingdom of the world, which is dominated by the work of the enemy. We can once again enjoy exceptional work – every day looking forward to our occupation. We can expect that our marriages will become exceptional in all aspects. We can trust God for exceptional provision. That beautiful, exceptional communion with God, once lost, can be restored to surpass what Adam had in the beginning. Praise God and thank him for washing your sin away! Receive the reconciliation to the Father through the Son. Embrace the cross and be forever changed.

CHAPTER 13
OUR RESPONSIBILITY TO FORGIVE

When we embrace the cross and the Lamb who died upon the cross, and when we receive forgiveness and reconciliation from the Father, we are forever changed. Indeed the old has gone and the new has come. And yet, there is a great and joyful responsibility given to us as we interact with our world as these new creations. We are called to forgive others as God has forgiven us. Is this difficult to do? No, it is impossible to do apart from the Spirit doing it in and through us!

You see, there is a critical truth regarding our ability to forgive others: If God operated and acted solely upon what we deserve, we would all experience eternal separation from God with no hope of ever having a relationship with the Father. The only reason we have the possibility of reconciliation is His nature of forgiveness. So, forgiveness is only available for us to receive and give away because of His nature. We love, because He first loved us. We forgive, because He first forgave us. This is important as we explore what this means in our everyday life. Forgiveness is not letting someone off the hook, because they satisfied some requirement of ours. Forgiveness is God's nature in us, operating toward another person who deserves our wrath and anger. It is actually not between you and another person, but it is ultimately between you and God – His Spirit and nature living in you.

OUR RESPONSIBILITY TO FORGIVE

To simply break things down:

1. If God forgave based upon what we deserve, then eternal unforgiveness and separation would necessarily ensue.

2. If God's forgiveness were dependent upon us doing better, trying harder, or attempting good works, then eternal unforgiveness and separation would be inevitable.

3. If God based His forgiveness of us upon us asking for a pardon as we would from a kind and generous judge, then eternal unforgiveness and separation would be the sentence.

We must fully understand and internalize the truth that forgiveness has nothing – absolutely nothing – to do with our response. Divine forgiveness rests fully upon God's nature; He is forgiveness. Without this nature, without this forgiveness, there is no possibility of reconciliation to the Father whatsoever. Through Christ's death and subsequent glorious resurrection, everyone has already been forgiven. He died once for us all, and the work demanded of Christ is indeed finished, completed. Because the work has already been done – since the guilt and wages of sin has been forever atoned for– Jesus has absolutely no difficulty nor struggle in extending forgiveness to anyone, even you. It matters not your past, your present circumstances, your gender, your race or your creed. Jesus offers this wonderful gift to all of mankind. Put your mind at ease, friend. You are free to run to Jesus and accept this beautiful gift, just as you are right now. You are not required to fix all of your mistakes or get all of your proverbial ducks in a row before being acceptable to Him. In fact, it is impossible to do so.

The forgiveness offered to you accepts you just as you are and is given by one who loves you just as you are and more than you could comprehend. There is no partiality in God's family, either. God's forgiveness is full and complete – there are no "second class citizens" in the Kingdom. He extends forgiveness and reconciliation to you, even if you are guilty, even if you are grieving, and even if you are not able to correct your mistakes or are incapable of forgetting your past failures. You do not have to perform in order for him to notice you or to earn your way in any shape or form. Remember, this gift is based not upon our ability to do the right things or obey God's law; it is a gift freely bestowed upon those who don't deserve.

Based upon these words, you might be asking yourself how quickly can you experience God's forgiveness? God's Word tells us that it is instantaneous:

"If we confess our sins, He is faithful and righteous to forgive us our sins and to cleanse us from all unrighteousness." 1 John 1:9

How is this possible? Again, it is not based upon what we do, but upon His nature and what He has already done. The Almighty God is by nature forgiving and offers forgiveness endlessly to all his human creation – every moment, all the time, every time.

Once we understand that forgiveness is neither a human quality nor something that we actually "do," but rather it is God Himself and something we "receive," we can then begin to comprehend we are able to forgive everyone 100% of the time. This is only possible because forgiveness is not actually between me and another person,

OUR RESPONSIBILITY TO FORGIVE

but rather between me and God, who has already forgiven everyone. The work of forgiveness has already been completed, and because His forgiveness is complete and present, this forgiveness can flow through us to others who have wronged us. This happens on the same basis that he forgave us: God's nature. It's not based on what we deserve or what others deserve from us, but forgiveness is based on His own nature and the work He completed on the cross.

Be further encouraged by stories from scripture. God's word gives us example after example of those who deserved God's wrath, but instead experienced God's forgiveness:

Noah was known as a drunk, but God used him mightily.

Abraham lied about who his wife really was, but God gave him the covenant.

Jacob also lied and even stole his brother's inheritance, but God changed his name to Israel.

Moses disobeyed God and had a speech impediment, but he was used to lead the Israelites out of Egypt.

David did his share of sinning, but he was still known as a man after God's own heart.

Peter denied Jesus and had a temper, but he led thousands to the Lord.

Paul originally killed Christians, but God used him mightily to reach the Gentiles.

These are but a few of the imperfect humans who did things

that deserved God's wrath, but because of God's nature, received His forgiveness instead. They were all able to live an intimate life of joy with the Father.

Now, since God's nature is forgiveness, what about all the people in Scripture that did not enjoy His forgiveness? How is this possible even though we have already said all have been forgiven? How do these two truths reconcile? It all has to do with reconciliation. Reconciliation is not forgiveness and forgiveness is not reconciliation. It takes two parties to receive forgiveness and to be reconciled. God has no problem with forgiveness – He has forgiven all, but not all have responded to the truth and gift offered to them. Because of this, they remain unreconciled to God. First of all, how have you responded to God's gift of forgiveness? Have you received it personally? If so, then you are fully reconciled to God – rejoice! Since it is our call to forgive others, revisit that list of individuals you had compiled at the beginning of the book. Have you come to the point of forgiving some of them? Any of them? All of them? Forgiveness is a choice based upon God's nature and based upon His work already done in you. You may not feel like forgiving these people, but I encourage you to forgive them in spite of your feelings. Make the choice now to forgive, based upon the work of Christ and based upon Christ living within you; and let all that bitterness, anger, and guilt go. Take as long as you need to, but do not neglect this vital step to living in the fullness and abundance of the Kingdom.

CHAPTER 14
DEFINING RECONCILIATION

God is forgiving; forgiveness is at the core of His nature. God cannot help but to forgive, because He has already finished the work required towards us who deserve nothing but His wrath and eternal separation. The work done on the cross, once for all of us, was and is still very powerful. That work alone is what gives separated and estranged humanity hope of a relationship with a Holy and wholly separate and unique God. So, the key question is this: Do all people automatically experience this forgiveness? The answer is no. Even though God has already forgiven all of humanity because of the cross and has no hesitation about to whom He offers it, such forgiveness does not automatically translate into reconciliation. Why doesn't all of humanity experience God's forgiveness? Because forgiveness can only be experienced through true reconciliation. Think about it. When there is a conflict between two people or groups of people, forgiveness is offered by one side because their desire is to once more have a relationship with the other. Each side must process through the offense and hurt done to get to a point where each is able to move on and let go of their anger and frustration. Both parties' expectations for continuing in relationship must be satisfied. Such actions and resolved tension lead to a deeper relationship, and a deeper trust and respect is experienced. Without forgiveness, a relationship cannot exist. Without trust, no relationship can stand.

LIFE IN FORGIVENESS

The Truth Regarding Forgiveness and Reconciliaton

So what is the truth that satisfies Christ's offer of forgiveness to be reconciled to Him? Good question ... but first we must revisit who God is and look again at His nature. God is holy. God is "wholly other" than his creation, and since this is true, we must understand He requires holiness and perfect righteousness of all who come into His presence. Because of His holiness, He neither can come in contact nor associate with unholiness and unrighteousness – in essence, ungodliness. It is no surprise that we cannot attain to such a high expectations. Scripture says all men and women have fallen short of this requirement, thusly deserving of His wrath and unforgiveness. We stand condemned already; we stand eternally separated already; and we stand hopeless already ... but there is hope. Christ has already performed the necessary requirements to satisfy God's demands of holiness and righteousness. He offers His perfect life for our imperfect one, and His horrible death in exchange for our impending death. His death leads to our life. In order to receive, we have to believe this beautiful gift offered to us is true in the deepest part of ourselves, our heart – our soul. When this happens, our condemnation is substituted for life abundant, and we are reconciled to God forever. If we do not believe, we remain condemned; we remain separated from God; and we remain hopeless and reconciliation cannot be attained.

"...so that whoever believes will in Him have eternal life. For God so loved the world, that He gave His only begotten Son, that

DEFINING RECONCILIATION

whoever believes in Him shall not perish, but have eternal life. For God did not send the Son into the world to judge the world, but that the world might be saved through Him. He who believes in Him is not judged; he who does not believe has been judged already, because he has not believed in the name of the only begotten Son of God." John 3:15-18

"Truly, truly, I say to you, he who hears My word, and believes Him who sent Me, has eternal life, and does not come into judgment, but has passed out of death into life." John 5:24

"For this reason also, since the day we heard of it, we have not ceased to pray for you and to ask that you may be filled with the knowledge of His will in all spiritual wisdom and understanding, so that you will walk in a manner worthy of the Lord, to please Him in all respects, bearing fruit in every good work and increasing in the knowledge of God; strengthened with all power, according to His glorious might, for the attaining of all steadfastness and patience; joyously giving thanks to the Father, who has qualified us to share in the inheritance of the saints in Light. For He rescued us from the domain of darkness, and transferred us to the kingdom of His beloved Son, in whom we have redemption, the forgiveness of sins. He is the image of the invisible God, the firstborn of all creation. For by Him all things were created, both in the heavens and on earth, visible and invisible, whether thrones or dominions or rulers or authorities— all things have been created through Him and for Him. He is before all things,

and in Him all things hold together. He is also head of the body, the church; and He is the beginning, the firstborn from the dead, so that He Himself will come to have first place in everything. For it was the Father's good pleasure for all the fullness to dwell in Him, and through Him to reconcile all things to Himself, having made peace through the blood of His cross; through Him, I say, whether things on earth or things in heaven. And although you were formerly alienated and hostile in mind, engaged in evil deeds, yet He has now reconciled you in His fleshly body through death, in order to present you before Him holy and blameless and beyond reproach— if indeed you continue in the faith firmly established and steadfast, and not moved away from the hope of the gospel that you have heard, which was proclaimed in all creation under heaven, and of which I, Paul, was made a minister" Colossians 1:9-23

This begs the question: Does Christ alter any of this truth in order to be reconciled to humanity? Absolutely not! As forgiving and desirous as Christ is in order to be reconciled to His creation, He in no way alters the truth set forth in His Word. Christ is, always has been, and always will be the only way to be reconciled with God.

> *"Jesus said to him, 'I am the way, and the truth, and the life; no one comes to the Father but through Me.'"* John 14:6

> *"He who believes in the Son has eternal life; but he who does not obey the Son will not see life, but the wrath of God abides on him."* John 3:36

DEFINING RECONCILIATION

"He who has the Son has the life; he who does not have the Son of God does not have the life." 1 John 5:12

Amidst all of the beauty and hope and relief experienced in the realization of the forgiveness offered to us, there is a hard truth to accept and know. In order to maintain His holiness and perfection, Christ will allow His creation, humanity, not to be reconciled and remain eternally separated from God, even though the work of forgiveness has been finished. This is a tough concept to comprehend, and prevents many from accepting such a beautiful gift. Many people cannot accept a loving and forgiving God who does not automatically forgive all of his creation. However, truth must be maintained in order for it to remain truth. God's truth must be able to stand on its own, independently, and cannot change in order for God to remain true to His nature of being completely holy and righteous. Where would we be if God changed His mind or requirements for appeasing His wrath on a case-by-case basis? We would be dealing with a being much like ourselves, not a God who is wholly other and different from His creation. We must first be relegated to the fact that humanity is, by nature, unrighteous, unholy, and permanently separated from God, who is completely righteous and holy. The conundrum presented between separated humanity and God's desire to reconcile has but one solution. Christ is the only remedy and the only way to bridge that separation. The only part we play is to believe and receive the work Christ has already accomplished on the cross on our behalf. Christ Himself does not alter the truth He died for … the truth He lived for. Through His compassion, Christ allows reconciliation but still stands firmly on the redemptive work done through His death, burial, and resurrection. It is this work which allows Him to freely offer the opportunity for reconciliation to all of mankind.

> *"Therefore let us be diligent to enter that rest, so that no one will fall, through following the same example of disobedience. For the word of God is living and active and sharper than any two-edged sword, and piercing as far as the division of soul and spirit, of both joints and marrow, and able to judge the thoughts and intentions of the heart. And there is no creature hidden from His sight, but all things are open and laid bare to the eyes of Him with whom we have to do."* Hebrews 4:11-13

> *"Nevertheless many even of the rulers believed in Him, but because of the Pharisees they were not confessing Him, for fear that they would be put out of the synagogue; for they loved the approval of men rather than the approval of God. And Jesus cried out and said, 'He who believes in Me, does not believe in Me but in Him who sent Me. He who sees Me sees the One who sent Me. I have come as Light into the world, so that everyone who believes in Me will not remain in darkness. If anyone hears My sayings and does not keep them, I do not judge him; for I did not come to judge the world, but to save the world. He who rejects Me and does not receive My sayings, has one who judges him; the word I spoke is what will judge him at the last day. For I did not speak on My own initiative, but the Father Himself who sent Me has given Me a commandment as to what to say*

DEFINING RECONCILIATION

and what to speak. I know that His commandment is eternal life; therefore the things I speak, I speak just as the Father has told Me.'" John 12:42-50

So, the gift of forgiveness must be believed in and then fully received and accepted in order for reconciliation and all of its benefits to be experienced. Again, the truth stands on its own. Christ has a heart and compassion for all to be reconciled to him, just like 2 Peter 3:9 says:

"The Lord is not slow about His promise, as some count slowness, but is patient toward you, not wishing for any to perish but for all to come to repentance."

Does this mean Christ will let us NOT be reconciled to God, and therefore, eternally separated from Him – even though He has finished the work of forgiveness? Yes. Remember, reconciliation requires truth to be accepted – and Christ does not alter the truth in order that a person may accept a partial element of truth to achieve reconciliation. What is this truth? It's the unalterable truth found in Christ. Although He has completely forgiven all and continually offers reconciliation to all, not all will be reconciled because of their unwillingness to receive it, process through it, and believe upon it. As a result, those that do not process the truth of their own sinfulness, believe in Christ's redemptive work, and receive His forgiveness will spend eternity unreconciled and will live eternally separated in hell from the Father, Son and Holy Spirit.

Who are the people you know who are not reconciled to the

LIFE IN FORGIVENESS

Father? Who among your friends and family members have yet to believe and receive the unconditional love and forgiveness offered by Christ? With such a vitally important question hanging in the balance, prayerfully consider how to ask this question to your friends and family. Ask for wisdom and boldness as you embark on sharing with others how the cross of Christ has changed you. Forgiveness and reconciliation to God is amazingly good news, so share it joyfully and see where God takes you on your journey.

CHAPTER 15
TRUTH OF SEPARATION

The questions raised at the end of the previous chapter are all well and good, but what about those of us who have been reconciled, through accepting and believing His truth? This topic of being disconnected and estranged comes into the believer's mind from time to time, and some of those times we have questions about forgiveness and reconciliation. For instance, is there any way believers can be separated from God again? Can children of God be unreconciled again, and consequently, not experience His fellowship? Eternally speaking … the answer is no.

> *"Truly, truly, I say to you, he who hears My word, and believes Him who sent Me, has eternal life, and does not come into judgment, but has passed out of death into life."* John 5:24

> *"And the testimony is this, that God has given us eternal life, and this life is in His Son. He who has the Son has the life; he who does not have the Son of God does not have the life."* 1 John 5:11-12

> *"For no man can lay a foundation other than the one which is laid, which is Jesus Christ. Now if any man builds on the foundation with gold, silver, precious stones, wood, hay, straw, each man's work will become evident; for the day will show it*

> because it is to be revealed with fire, and the fire itself will test the quality of each man's work. If any man's work which he has built on it remains, he will receive a reward. If any man's work is burned up, he will suffer loss; but he himself will be saved, yet so as through fire." 1 Corinthians 3:11-15

It is incredibly encouraging to know that once we are reconciled to God through His gift of forgiveness, we are forever so reconciled. Nothing can alter our changed position. We have received his forgiveness and are reconciled, and nothing can separate us from God's love.

Regarding Believers Now

Remember the questions in the previous section:

Is there any way believers can be separated from God again?

Can children of God be unreconciled again, and consequently, not experience His fellowship?

Eternally speaking, we now know that the answer is no. However, we must understand that we can experience separation from God's fellowship in the present.

> "For those who are according to the flesh set their minds on the things of the flesh, but those who are according to the Spirit, the things of the Spirit. For the mind set on the flesh is death, but the mind set on the Spirit is life and peace, because the mind set on the flesh is hostile toward God; for it does not subject itself to the law of God, for it is not even able to do so, and those who are in the flesh cannot please God." Romans 8:5-8

TRUTH OF SEPARATION

"Yet they tempted and rebelled against the Most High God and did not keep His testimonies, but turned back and acted treacherously like their fathers; they turned aside like a treacherous bow. For they provoked Him with their high places and aroused His jealousy with their graven images. When God heard, He was filled with wrath and greatly abhorred Israel; so that He abandoned the dwelling place at Shiloh, the tent which He had pitched among men, and gave up His strength to captivity And His glory into the hand of the adversary. He also delivered His people to the sword, and was filled with wrath at His inheritance. Fire devoured His young men, and His virgins had no wedding songs. His priests fell by the sword, and His widows could not weep." Psalm 78:56-64

"Behold, the Lord's hand is not so short that it cannot save; nor is His ear so dull that it cannot hear. But your iniquities have made a separation between you and your God, and your sins have hidden His face from you so that He does not hear. For your hands are defiled with blood and your fingers with iniquity; your lips have spoken falsehood, your tongue mutters wickedness. No one sues righteously and no one pleads honestly. They trust in confusion and speak lies; they conceive mischief and bring forth iniquity." Isaiah 59:1-4

We as believers can be separated from God due to our iniquity, or sin, even though our eternal salvation is secure. Our unwillingness to walk in the Spirit and surrender our will to His will separates us from God's life and His fellowship. When this happens, we are in a position of being unreconciled (loss of fellowship) within the moment. In addition, when those circumstances arise putting the flesh before the Spirit, we also experience the three consequences of not being reconciled to God: quenching the spirit (killing the life of the Holy Spirit in our lives), being at enmity against God (where we work in opposition to His will and believe He works against us), and being unable to please God. If this is not serious enough, our choice to walk directed by the self (carnal mind) also prevents us from having our prayers heard by the Father, and we no longer live within the protection of His promises and benefits given to His reconciled children. We must be able to fully grasp these facts. A life lived in intimacy with God, fully receiving all of the benefits of being reconciled to the creator, does not come automatically. Instead, believers have a choice in how they live: one, either operating in the self, the carnal - as practical atheists and living a life independent of God and experiencing the consequences of that life; or two, living within the intimate community of and in relationship with the Father. This may explain why so many believers live oppressed, difficult, harsh and unpleasant lives … because they are unwilling to fully receive and live in forgiveness.

The Remedy is Embracing Truth

As just mentioned, those who have been reconciled – believers, followers of Christ – have a continual choice in how to live. If we choose to live in the Spirit, our relationship with God is close and nothing impedes communication between the two. However, if we do not choose to live in the Spirit, we are choosing by default to live in the flesh, in the self, and our relationship with God is temporarily broken. Once again, sin and self separate the creator from His creation, but it is only in terms of fellowship, not of position. Again, the remedy is simple. We need to be reconciled to His truth. We need reconciliation to God's heart. Once again, we must understand that He has already completed the work of forgiveness, and we are forgiven. This is no problem for Him, but for instant reconciliation, repentance and confession play a key role. It is essential to tell God how we have been walking according to the flesh and then repent of our behavior, and He will forgive us.

> *"If we confess our sins, He is faithful and righteous to forgive us our sins and to cleanse us from all unrighteousness."* 1 John 1:9

> *"Be gracious to me, O God, according to Your loving-kindness; according to the greatness of Your compassion blot out my transgressions. Wash me thoroughly from my iniquity and cleanse me from my sin. For I know my transgressions, and my sin is ever before me. Against You, You only, I have sinned and done what is evil in Your sight, so that You are justified when You speak and blameless when You judge. Behold, I was brought forth in iniquity, and in sin my mother conceived me. Behold, You desire truth in the innermost being, and in the hidden part You will make me know wisdom. Purify me with hyssop, and I shall be clean; wash me, and I shall be whiter than snow. Make me to hear joy and gladness, let the bones, which You have broken,*

rejoice. Hide Your face from my sins and blot out all my iniquities. Create in me a clean heart, O God, and renew a steadfast spirit within me. Do not cast me away from Your presence and do not take Your Holy Spirit from me. Restore to me the joy of Your salvation and sustain me with a willing spirit. Then I will teach transgressors Your ways, and sinners will be converted to You. Deliver me from blood-guiltiness, O God, the God of my salvation; then my tongue will joyfully sing of Your righteousness. O Lord, open my lips, that my mouth may declare Your praise. For You do not delight in sacrifice, otherwise I would give it; you are not pleased with burnt offering. The sacrifices of God are a broken spirit; a broken and a contrite heart, O God, You will not despise. By Your favor do good to Zion; Build the walls of Jerusalem. Then You will delight in righteous sacrifices, in burnt offering and whole burnt offering; then young bulls will be offered on Your altar." Psalm 51

"and My people who are called by My name humble themselves and pray and seek My face and turn from their wicked ways, then I will hear from heaven, will forgive their sin and will heal their land. Now My eyes will be open and My ears attentive to the prayer offered in this place." 2 Chronicles 7:14-15

"Now, Israel, what does the Lord your God require from you, but to fear the Lord your God, to walk in all His ways and love Him, and to serve the Lord your God with all your heart and with all your soul, and to keep the Lord's commandments and His stat-

TRUTH OF SEPARATION

utes which I am commanding you today for your good? Behold, to the Lord your God belong heaven and the highest heavens, the earth and all that is in it." Deuteronomy 10:12-14

Throughout these scriptures, we are told to "fear God" and that this fear of the Almighty is required in our repentance. However, the fear described here needs an explanation. Most of the time when we fear something, such fears are defined as one being scared, having dread towards something, or fear causing anxiety. When scripture tells us to fear God, it in no means intends for us to have dread towards God. God is loving and forgiving. Remember how we talked about His nature? That he cannot help but forgive? That God is Holy? According to the definition of the Hebrew word, the fear of the Lord means to stand in awe of, to revere, and to honor and respect God. This is done when we acknowledge our Creator as all powerful, all mighty, and all knowing and that we are not. This acknowledgement of God's position and character puts us in our rightful position of needing His wisdom, power, care, and forgiveness. In short, we recognize we cannot live apart from Him or from the Spirit. Fearing God also means we believe His Word is true and that all He speaks through His word is true and available to us all. Stop debating and doubting whether or not what you hear from the Word is true; and instead, process the confusion and questions further with God until clarity is experienced. Then stand in awe and reverence of God the most holy and recognize that by following His Word, you will receive blessings; but a refusal to hear and follow will lead to negative consequences.

Next, we are told to walk in God's ways. In order to do this, we must choose to die to our self (our self-agenda, our self-centeredness, etc.) and allow God's Spirit to work through us and live fully in us. When we choose to walk with Him instead of our own selfish ways; when we surrender our will to His will; when we desire to truly hear what He wants to say to us; then we can walk in God's ways. Then we are able to follow Him as he leads and guides us, step by step, day by day, and we can remain on His path, not our own. Denying our flesh, following God's instructions for our life, and surrendering our will to Christ's is how we live life to the fullest – the abundant life Jesus came to give! Is it difficult? Denying of our flesh certainly does not come naturally, but the more we do it, the easier it becomes to follow Christ. Here is an example:

At one of our retreats, there was a young couple who had been married a few years. The husband was a financial planner, and she was an aspiring country music songwriter. She would travel back and forth to Nashville attempting to break into the business, and he worked hard to build his local practice. They wanted to have children but were waiting. They felt as though their financial position would not allow them to manage a family, and they were unsure of where to put down roots with so many questions about work, family, etc. They had a strained marriage but not because they were angry at each other. Instead, the strain was experienced because they each had a concept of what life should be like, but they were not taking the time to work it through together until reaching a consensus. No couple can learn to walk with God in the Spirit with unresolved conflict or unfulfilled expectations festering in their souls. At all of our retreats

TRUTH OF SEPARATION

we spend significant time discussing how to abide in Christ, how to walk in the Spirit, how to surrender our will to His, and how to seek His best for us. There at the retreat, they agreed they had been living their lives engaged in their own self-centeredness. Upon this realization, they decided to learn a new way, which included surrendering their will to the Father's. What happened first was they were released of the pressure of trying to figure everything out. They decided to live life in unity - on the same side of the table - and to have God reveal and show His will to them. They began enjoying, abiding, sharing the truths that God was revealing to them, and seeking the wisdom of God in all their decisions. For two years God revealed His will to them step by step. The wife received an international songwriting contract from a firm located in Los Angeles, and his work continued to thrive locally. Because of the opportunities from her new management company, she is fully endorsed and able to establish roots in their hometown. They are cleared by God to begin a family. They have been led to sell the condo (which sold the first day listed), and they bought a new home in the suburbs. Their marriage is continuing to flourish as they together abide in the vine and walk in the Spirit. Their life has changed to one full of joy and wonder, and they are beginning to "give it away" to their friends who have seen the change in their life and have a desire to learn what it means to walk in the Spirit. This is all because they made a decision to surrender their will to God, deny themselves, and taking up the cross to follow Him.

Was it difficult for this couple to deny their self-will, both individually and collectively? Any time anyone denies his flesh, a struggle will ensue. However, this couple made a choice to leave the decision making to God in their marriage and in their lives, and it was worth every struggle. So, yes, denying the self is hard, but in comparison with the joy of following Christ in an intimate and abiding relationship, there is no sorrow. However, denial of the flesh is only one aspect of following Christ.

Another important aspect of walking with God is to love God with all of our heart and soul. We know that even that is impossible apart from Christ fully living within us; and us making that conscious decision to walk in the Spirit. Walking every moment in this place naturally develops that deep affection towards being with Christ, caring for Him, and simply enjoying His presence and His affection towards you – His dearly loved child. Such affection and love is communicated through communion, prayer, scripture reading, etc. Basically the more time you choose to walk in the Spirit, the more you fall in love with Jesus. The more you fall in love with Jesus, the more time you will spend with Him, talking with Him. The more time you spend with Him, the more you will choose to walk in the Spirit and be led and guided by it. Eventually you get to the point where you ask yourself, "In light of how much He loves me and I love Him, why would I do anything else?"

What else are we to do as Christ followers? We are called to serve our King. When you walk in the Spirit, you see your role as serving God and His desires, instead of your own will. When we have a heart already surrendered to His will, our servant's heart will desire nothing more than to join Him where He is at work. Knowing fully His will

TRUTH OF SEPARATION

and His direction for your life, is better than anything we could ever imagine. And finally, God calls us to follow His instructions. While living a life directed by God's Spirit living within you, you will gain a heart of obedience to follow God's commands as it relates to you personally. To the best of your ability, you take each step laid before you in faith, knowing the promises associated with each step of obedience will be fulfilled by the promise keeper.

This is a big area of consternation for most believers. We are taught that in order to receive God's favor, we must be obedient and follow the precepts and instructions in Scripture. We think if we were able to perform a good portion of God's precepts (we know we cannot keep them all), we can then hope we are good enough to obtain blessings and favor. We still see God as a lawgiver, distant from us, requiring us to be holy and righteous. We have it all backwards. Righteousness is Christ, and we can only become righteous by putting on Christ. Furthermore, holiness is a fruit of the Spirit, not something we achieve; rather, it is a result of our relationship with Christ. Romans chapter 6 gives us an interesting progression regarding experiencing holiness. Verse 7 says, *"for he who has died has been freed from sin"* – done deal, past tense. Verse 18 builds upon that and says, *"and having been set free from sin, you became slaves of righteousness."* We surrendered our will to His, and have an intimate relationship with Him. Verse 22 completes the progression: *"But now having been set free from sin, and having become slaves of God, you have your fruit to holiness, and the end, everlasting life."* Holiness is a result of our living life freed from sin through his forgiveness, and then us surrendering our lives to Him with a heart to serve Him completely. As we do, we then have a love and a relationship to follow him, knowing that His will is best, and there is none better. Our love grows, our intimacy grows, and our obedience is fulfilled through His power in us and out of our love for him. It is much like that of a toddler to his parents. A toddler naturally has affection for his parents, and through the loving instruction and care of the parents, learns to willingly obey the parents' instructions. He or she quickly learns that things go better when he or she obeys his parents. In the same way, obeying the Father is a true joy and is done out of our heart relationship, not as a duty.

So, how is your walk with the Father? Are you walking in that joyful experience which is an abiding relationship in the vine? Are you presently separated from a close relationship with God? If so, there is wonderful news for you … you can have a restored and reconciled relationship beginning right now! Repent and turn from your flesh, from the self, and turn towards God in faith and trust. Walk in the Spirit one step at a time, one day at a time, and get up every time you fall. This is the beginning of life's greatest adventure and fulfillment.

CHAPTER 16
WALKING HOPE FOR WANDERERS

So, let's say you have wandered away from walking in the Spirit, and your sin has separated you from the fellowship of God you once experienced. Now what? The answer is the same: repent and believe. Once we admit our sin to God and confess how we have missed the mark God set for us, He will forgive us, because He is faithful to His word and promises. Our fellowship with our Creator is completely restored. Is this restoration always available? Yes. How many times can we possibly expect to be forgiven of our sin and shortcomings? God's forgiveness is endless. He will forgive us as many times as we sincerely ask for it.

> *"Then Peter came and said to Him, 'Lord, how often shall my brother sin against me and I forgive him? Up to seven times?' Jesus said to him, 'I do not say to you, up to seven times, but up to seventy times seven.'"* Matthew 18:21-22

This is an interesting passage. Jewish tradition taught people to forgive their offenders three times and no more. So when Peter spoke the number seven, more than double the number expected of a "good Jewish man," he was asking if human forgiveness should be exercised to such a great extent. The number seven also had spiritual connotations, meaning the fullness of perfection. So, in a way, Peter was also asking what was the perfect solution to how often should man be forgiven by another. Jesus' response spoke of God's offering of forgiveness to humanity, and our reply as mere humans in turn. The seventy times seven reference denotes an endless supply of God's forgiveness towards us, His creation. And since He first forgave us, we are to offer endless forgiveness to those who offend us. In a simple mathematical equation, Jesus confounded the wisdom of Jewish tradition by multiplying the expectation for our reaction to wrongs done to us far beyond what anyone had previously thought. And the reason for such a shockingly large number? Because God forgives us all the more. Remember, because God is faithful and just, he cleanses us instantaneously (1 John 1:9) each and every time He forgives us; and therefore, there is nothing for us to fix. We need to merely return and be restored. Christ tells us there are no limits to His forgiveness. It is day by day, moment by moment, and there is endless opportunity to be reconciled. So how does this apply to everyday life for you and me?

If you had a brother or sister who agreed to meet you for lunch and then failed to show up, you would certainly be upset but probably forgive them. If it happened a second time, you would be more upset but could probably forgive them again. However, if it happened a third time, we would basically say, "That's enough, I am done with this," and we would struggle to forgive them yet again, right? In our natural life, we have limitations as to how much we can take. Perhaps this will help us understand the depth of Christ's nature – endless forgiveness with no limitations. And if He has endless forgiveness toward us, through Him, we can have endless forgiveness toward others.

WALKING HOPE FOR WANDERERS

Experiencing Restoration

How does this relate to reconciliation? We recall that Christ never alters the truth in order for us to experience restoration and reconciliation. We can stay unreconciled and live outside of an intimate relationship with Him, outside of the benefits of living in this relationship.

> *"While it is said, 'Today if you hear His voice, do not harden your hearts, as when they provoked Me.' For who provoked Him when they had heard? Indeed, did not all those who came out of Egypt led by Moses? And with whom was He angry for forty years? Was it not with those who sinned, whose bodies fell in the wilderness? And to whom did He swear that they would not enter His rest, but to those who were disobedient? So we see that they were not able to enter because of unbelief."* Hebrews 3:15-19

The Israelites, who had been "saved" through the parting of the Red Sea, were given a promise by God. His will was for them to enter the Promised Land, and He told the Israelites He would defeat their enemies and deliver them into all of the benefits of living in the Promised Land. However, they refused to go because of fear. They refused to believe God would fulfill His promises, and it was this unbelief, which led to God's anger towards them. God was angry with that generation and allowed them to wander in the wilderness for forty years and refused to let the unfaithful enter into the land He had promised. Those people died outside of the good and perfect will of God. God in no way altered the truth so that generation could enter into the Promised Land. Those

LIFE IN FORGIVENESS

Israelites were not willing to fully process the truth of God's promises despite their fear, and they remained unreconciled to God and suffered the consequences of such. However, God did not abandon His chosen people. He provided His presence in a cloud by day and a pillar of fire by night, both for their protection. He gave them manna each morning, quail to eat, plenty of water to drink, and neither their clothing nor their shoes ever wore out – for forty years! God still provided for them, because He never stopped loving them. Their status as God's chosen people was secure, just like our eternal salvation is secure upon our initial repenting and believing; but they lived their lives apart from the intimate relationship God offered them and wanted to have with them. Instead, they lived out the remainder of their years wandering around aimlessly in the wilderness and never received the promises God spoke to them. God offered reconciliation, but they did not receive the offer, and therefore, reconciliation never happened. Reconciliation necessitates that two parties both process truth and come to a resolution satisfactory to and accepted by both parties. With this, reconciliation happens. Without it, reconciliation will not happen.

Have you received this reconciliation from God? Are there others in your life you need to offer reconciliation to today? Remember, we are called to offer forgiveness to others as Christ offers forgiveness to the world – at all times and without condition. Regarding those who have hurt you, pray for God to give you the strength to forgive them, and then forgive them. Do not allow your self-will to rule. Walk in God's Spirit and forgive them in His power, releasing them to God. Through this act, you are opening yourself up to absolute freedom with the Father

CHAPTER 17
BENEFITS OF RECONCILIATION

What, if any, are the **benefits of reconciliation**, other than avoiding the consequences experienced by not being reconciled to Him?

- **We Receive Redemption – Life in Exchange for Death.**

"In Him we have redemption through His blood, the forgiveness of our trespasses, according to the riches of His grace which He lavished on us. In all wisdom and insight He made known to us the mystery of His will, according to His kind intention which He purposed in Him with a view to an administration suitable to the fullness of the times, that is, the summing up of all things in Christ, things in the heavens and things on the earth. In Him also we have obtained an inheritance, having been predestined according to His purpose who works all things after the counsel of His will, to the end that we who were the first to hope in Christ would be to the praise of His glory." Ephesians 1:7-12

"For consider your calling, brethren, that there were not many wise according to the flesh, not many mighty, not many noble; but God has chosen the foolish things of the world to shame the wise, and God has chosen the weak things of the world to shame the things which are strong, and the base things of the world and the despised God has chosen, the things that are not, so that He

may nullify the things that are, so that no man may boast before God. But by His doing you are in Christ Jesus, who became to us wisdom from God, and righteousness and sanctification, and redemption, so that, just as it is written, 'Let him who boasts, boast in the Lord.'" 1 Corinthians 1:26-31

"The thief comes only to steal and kill and destroy; I came that they may have life, and have it abundantly." John 10:10

- **We Receive His Righteousness.**

"If we confess our sins, He is faithful and righteous to forgive us our sins and to cleanse us from all unrighteousness." 1 John 1:9

"…for all have sinned and fall short of the glory of God, being justified as a gift by His grace through the redemption which is in Christ Jesus; whom God displayed publicly as a propitiation in His blood through faith. This was to demonstrate His righteousness, because in the forbearance of God He passed over the sins previously committed; for the demonstration, I say, of His righteousness at the present time, so that He would be just and the justifier of the one who has faith in Jesus." Romans 3:23-26

- **We Receive His Guidance.**

"I will instruct you and teach you in the way which you should go; I will counsel you with My eye upon you. Do not be as the horse or as the mule, that have no understanding, whose trappings

BENEFITS OF RECONCILIATION

include bit and bridle to hold them in check, otherwise they will not come near to you. Many are the sorrows of the wicked, but he who trusts in the Lord, loving-kindness shall surround him. Be glad in the Lord and rejoice, you righteous ones; and shout for joy, all you who are upright in heart." Psalm 32:8-9

"But if any of you lacks wisdom, let him ask of God, who gives to all generously and [a]without reproach, and it will be given to him." James 1:5

"Trust in the Lord with all your heart and do not lean on your own understanding. In all your ways acknowledge Him, and He will make your paths straight." Proverbs 3:5-6

- **We Receive Joy and Pleasure.**

  "You will make known to me the path of life; in Your presence is fullness of joy; in Your right hand there are pleasures forever." Psalm 16:11

  "Many are the sorrows of the wicked, but he who trusts in the Lord, loving-kindness shall surround him. Be glad in the Lord and rejoice, you righteous ones; and shout for joy, all you who are upright in heart." Psalm 32:10-11

  "Thus says the Lord, 'Let not a wise man boast of his wisdom, and let not the mighty man boast of his might, let not a rich man boast of his riches; but let him who boasts boast of this, that he understands and knows Me, that I am the Lord who exercises

loving-kindness, justice and righteousness on earth; for I delight in these things,' declares the Lord." Jeremiah 9:23-24

"The afflicted also will increase their gladness in the Lord, and the needy of mankind will rejoice in the Holy One of Israel." Isaiah 29:19

- **He Forgets our Failure.**

"As far as the east is from the west, so far has He removed our transgressions from us. Just as a father has compassion on his children, so the Lord has compassion on those who fear Him." Psalm 103:12-13

"This is the covenant that I will make with them after those days, says the Lord: 'I will put My laws upon their heart, and on their mind I will write them,' He then says, 'And their sins and their lawless deeds I will remember no more.' Now where there is forgiveness of these things, there is no longer any offering for sin." Hebrews 10:16-18

"For I will be merciful to their iniquities, and I will remember their sins no more." Hebrews 8:12

- **We Receive Power.**

"In Him, you also, after listening to the message of truth, the gospel of your salvation – having also believed, you were sealed in Him with the Holy Spirit of promise, who is given as a pledge

BENEFITS OF RECONCILIATION

of our inheritance, with a view to the redemption of God's own possession, to the praise of His glory. For this reason I too, having heard of the faith in the Lord Jesus which exists among you and your love for all the saints, do not ceases giving thanks for you, while making mention of you in my prayers; that the God of our Lord Jesus Christ, the Father of glory, may give you a spirit of wisdom and of revelation in the knowledge of Him. I pray that the eyes of your heart may be enlightened, so that you will know what is the hope of His calling, what are the riches of the glory of His inheritance in the saints, and what is the surpassing greatness of his power toward us who believe. These are in accordance with the working of the strength of his might which He brought about in Christ, when He raised Him from the dead and seated Him at His right hand in the heavenly places, far above all rule and authority and power and dominion, and every name that is named not only in this age but also in the one to come. And He put all things in subjection under His feet, and gave Him as head over all things to the church, which is His body, the fullness of Him who fills all in all." Ephesians 1:13-23

"For this reason I bow my knees before the Father, from whom every family in heaven and on earth derives its name, that He would grant you, according to the riches of His glory, to be strengthened with power through His Spirit in the inner man, so that Christ may dwell in your hearts through faith; and that you, being rooted and grounded in love, may be able to comprehend with all the saints what is the breadth and length and height and

depth, and to know the love of Christ which surpasses knowledge, that you may be filled up to all the fullness of God. Now to Him who is able to do far more abundantly beyond all that we ask or think, according to the power that works within us, to Him be the glory in the church and in Christ Jesus to all generations forever and ever. Amen." Ephesians 3:14-21

- **We Receive His Peace.**

  ""These things I have spoken to you while abiding with you. But the Helper, the Holy Spirit, whom the Father will send in My name, He will teach you all things, and bring to your remembrance all that I said to you. Peace I leave with you; My peace I give to you; not as the world gives do I give to you. Do not let your heart be troubled, nor let it be fearful." John 14:25-27

  "These things I have spoken to you, so that in Me you may have peace. In the world you have tribulation, but take courage; I have overcome the world." John 16:33

  "The Lord will give strength to His people; the Lord will bless His people with peace." Psalm 29:11

- **We Receive Mercy, Kindness and Tenderness.**

  "Who redeems your life from the pit, who crowns you with loving-kindness and compassion…The Lord is compassionate and gracious, slow to anger and abounding in loving-kindness. He will not always strive with us, nor will He keep His anger forever.

BENEFITS OF RECONCILIATION

He has not dealt with us according to our sins, nor rewarded us according to our iniquities." Psalm 103:4, 8-10

"O Israel, hope in the Lord; for with the Lord there is loving-kindness, and with Him is abundant redemption. And He will redeem Israel from all his iniquities." Psalm 130:7-8

"The Lord's loving-kindnesses indeed never cease, for His compassions never fail. They are new every morning; great is Your faithfulness. 'The Lord is my portion,' says my soul, 'Therefore I have hope in Him.' The Lord is good to those who wait for Him, to the person who seeks Him. It is good that he waits silently for the salvation of the Lord." Lamentations 3:22-26

- **We Receive Healing.**
"Bless the Lord, O my soul, and all that is within me, bless His holy name. Bless the Lord, O my soul, and forget none of His benefits; who pardons all your iniquities, who heals all your diseases" Psalm 103:1-3

"O Lord my God, I cried to You for help, and You healed me." Psalm 30:2

"He heals the brokenhearted and binds up their wounds." Psalm 147:3

- **We are Delivered from Destructive Patterns.**
"Who redeems your life from the pit, who crowns you with loving-kindness and compassion." Psalm 103:4

LIFE IN FORGIVENESS

"The Lord will rescue me from every evil deed, and will bring me safely to His heavenly kingdom; to Him be the glory forever and ever. Amen." 2 Timothy 4:18

"God is to us a God of deliverances; and to God the Lord belong escapes from death." Psalm 68:20

- **We will be satisfied with good things.**

"Who satisfies your years with good things, so that your youth is renewed like the eagle." Psalm 103:5

"For He has satisfied the thirsty soul, and the hungry soul He has filled with what is good." Psalm 107:9

And these are just but a few of over 7,000 promises and benefits spoken to us and for us in Scripture.

God desires us to experience all of His goodness and rewards. After all, Jesus came into the world not to condemn it or to provide another list of tasks for us to accomplish, but He came to give us life and give it in abundance. God's nature is to desire for us to not only live life but to enjoy it to the fullest. When we live our lives in perpetual forgiveness towards others, we can live this abundant life and reap all of its benefits. In fact, living with such benefits is the very indication that we have been restored to a whole and immensely beautiful relationship with God. We become the living and walking testimonies of God's redemptive work offered to all of humanity. The same thing can be said of the benefits of living in restored relationships with our friends, families, and co-workers.

BENEFITS OF RECONCILIATION

When we are forgiven and live in the fullness of being forgiven, we can offer forgiveness freely to others. And yet, when we slip and live ruled by our flesh, our relationships with those around us are conflicted, jarred, and distant. We must remember to live with a Kingdom mentality. When we live Kingdom-minded, living as residents of a heavenly realm, we walk in the Spirit and experience the abundance of life available through our King. When we live according to self, we operate outside of the benefits, life, and protection of the Kingdom.

Take a moment to meditate on the Scriptures listed above. Allow God's truth to sink deeply into your heart, as you learn of the benefits of reconciliation. Listen to the Spirit, through God's Word, and let it whisper to you and give you life. Believe it, embrace it, and walk in its light.

CHAPTER 18
CALLING TO RECONCILE

Remember that in order for true reconciliation to occur between us and other people, we must first be reconciled to God. We must live out the simplicity of reconciliation – know that we are forgiven (already done and complete – no problem for Him), and then process through the truth that He offers to guide us until we reach agreement. Once reconciliation between us and God happens, then reconciliation between us and our offenders can take place on the same basis. We first forgive them, which is between us and God – on the same basis that He forgave us – by His nature. Then offer to process the truth, until we reach agreement, and thus, reconciliation. Remember, through living in the Spirit, we have the ability to forgive others, where in the flesh, we do not. When we receive and are abiding in His forgiving nature, we stand firm in the peace and freedom only God Himself can give. Walking in the liberty available through Christ only comes as a result of us being ready and willing to reconcile to God in the first place. Don't forget that we have to repent and believe. We have to believe God exists; that He is good; He wants to forgive us; and then we must accept the gift so unreservedly offered. However, if we continually refuse to seek the true reconciliation which only comes through forgiveness, living in God's peace and freedom will be unattainable. Reconciliation is not possible without forgiveness, and we then reap the consequences of unforgiveness.

CALLING TO RECONCILE

"Pursue peace with all men, and the sanctification without which no one will see the Lord. See to it that no one comes short of the grace of God; that no root of bitterness springing up causes trouble, and by it many be defiled; that there be no immoral or godless person like Esau, who sold his own birthright for a single meal. For you know that even afterwards, when he desired to inherit the blessing, he was rejected, for he found no place for repentance, though he sought for it with tears." Hebrews 12:14-17

"It was for freedom that Christ set us free; therefore keep standing firm and do not be subject again to a yoke of slavery. Behold I, Paul, say to you that if you receive circumcision, Christ will be of no benefit to you. And I testify again to every man who receives circumcision, that he is under obligation to keep the whole Law. You have been severed from Christ, you who are seeking to be justified by law; you have fallen from grace. For we through the Spirit, by faith, are waiting for the hope of righteousness. For in Christ Jesus neither circumcision nor uncircumcision means anything, but faith working through love… Now the deeds of the flesh are evident, which are: immorality, impurity, sensuality, idolatry, sorcery, enmities, strife, jealousy, outbursts of anger, disputes, dissensions, factions, envying, drunkenness, carousing, and things like these, of which I forewarn you, just as I have forewarned you, that those who practice such things will not inherit the kingdom of God." Galatians 5:1-6, 19-21

"Therefore God gave them over in the lusts of their hearts to

impurity, so that their bodies would be dishonored among them. For they exchanged the truth of God for a lie, and worshiped and served the creature rather than the Creator, who is blessed forever. Amen. For this reason God gave them over to degrading passions; for their women exchanged the natural function for that which is unnatural, and in the same way also the men abandoned the natural function of the woman and burned in their desire toward one another, men with men committing indecent acts and receiving in their own persons the due penalty of their error. And just as they did not see fit to acknowledge God any longer, God gave them over to a depraved mind, to do those things which are not proper, being filled with all unrighteousness, wickedness, greed, evil; full of envy, murder, strife, deceit, malice; they are gossips, slanderers, haters of God, insolent, arrogant, boastful, inventors of evil, disobedient to parents, without understanding, untrustworthy, unloving, unmerciful; and although they know the ordinance of God, that those who practice such things are worthy of death, they not only do the same, but also give hearty approval to those who practice them." Romans 1:24-32

When we maintain unforgiveness, our anger is maintained, not resolved, and bitterness is the evil result. This bitterness is a clear indication someone has chosen to live in the flesh, has not surrendered their will to the Father, and are not willing to walk with God on the path He has chosen for them. There are serious consequences to such behavior. Such a person, including us from time to time if we are honest, is again placed under the bondage of the law and is required to keep the entirety of it. Since no one can keep the entire law in and of themselves, they fall from God's grace and become estranged from the personal and intimate relationship with Christ. Only within that wonderful relationship can we have all of our needs provided for and the power received to live the life of forgiveness. When any believer chooses to walk by the flesh, ruled by the flesh, they develop characteristics indicative of the world: anger, wrath, evil speaking, hardness, deceitful, backbiting, arguers, etc., and their life is lived in a constant sense of disappointment, oppression and resignation. Think about it. How many of us have been in a group of our friends, or even in church, and have heard others gossiping about someone? How many times have you lost your temper getting your children ready to go to church? How about friendships lost over petty issues? Church splits over the color of carpet to go in the sanctuary?

Unfortunately these and many more are a result of not living and walking in the Spirit. Can you now see why forgiveness is such a crucial issue to resolve in your own life? No one intentionally wants to sabotage their own happiness, joy, and peace but those who refuse to forgive and continue to walk according to the flesh end up doing just that. Forgiveness is not something we simply do in order to meet any type of spiritual requirement, and it is certainly nothing we can accomplish on our own. Rather, forgiveness is an indicator of if and how we are walking with our Father and guided by the Spirit. Similarly, backbiting, being argumentative, harshness, and wrath are indicators of the opposite. When God's children are close to their Father and are living in the gift of forgiveness they have so eagerly received, that very nature of God living in us allows us to quickly and readily forgive others.

God's Call to His Children

God's call to us is to live a life of continual forgiveness, as well as constantly offer reconciliation to others. But remember, forgiveness is separate from reconciliation. Our part is to first forgive others on the same basis God has forgiven us, not based upon what humanity deserves. God's loving and forgiving nature gives us the power to maintain His forgiving character through us to be offered in all circumstances and to all around us. But when we live in such darkness because our flesh rules us, forgiveness cannot be offered to others. If we fail to stay connected to the author of forgiveness, then offering it is impossible. So, how do we know if we are living according to God's forgiving nature?

> *"So, as those who have been chosen of God, holy and beloved, put on a heart of compassion, kindness, humility, gentleness and patience; bearing with one another, and forgiving each other, whoever has a complaint against anyone; just as the Lord forgave you, so also should you. Beyond all these things put on love, which is the perfect bond of unity. Let the peace of Christ rule in your hearts, to which indeed you were called in one body; and be thankful. Let the word of Christ richly dwell within you, with all wisdom teaching and admonishing one another with psalms and hymns and spiritual songs, singing with thankfulness in your*

hearts to God. Whatever you do in word or deed, do all in the name of the Lord Jesus, giving thanks through Him to God the Father." Colossians 3:12-17

Simply explained … we will know by our actions and reactions. When we think about someone who has hurt us, or their name is brought up in conversation, and we no longer associate them with bitterness, we are walking in the Spirit. When we do not become angry or resentful of them for what they have done, we are walking in the Spirit. When we do not desire revenge or a need to withdraw from them, it is by the Spirit we are being led. When we know we are able to be in the same room with our offender and can remain in peace and freedom, God's Spirit is leading us. When we can intercede for the one who wounded us and genuinely pray for the best God has for them, we are walking in the Spirit. How do we know? Because all of those actions are a result of forgiving them the wrong they did to you.

> *"Now in a large house there are not only gold and silver vessels, but also vessels of wood and of earthenware, and some to honor and some to dishonor. Therefore, if anyone cleanses himself from these things, he will be a vessel for honor, sanctified, useful to the Master, prepared for every good work. Now flee from youthful lusts and pursue righteousness, faith, love and peace, with those who call on the Lord from a pure heart. But refuse foolish and ignorant speculations, knowing that they produce quarrels. The Lord's bond-servant must not be quarrelsome, but be kind to all, able to teach, patient when wronged, with gentleness correcting*

those who are in opposition, if perhaps God may grant them repentance leading to the knowledge of the truth, and they may come to their senses and escape from the snare of the devil, having been held captive by him to do his will." 2 Timothy 2:20-26

"Yield now and be at peace with Him; thereby good will come to you. Please receive instruction from His mouth and establish His words in your heart. If you return to the Almighty, you will be restored; if you remove unrighteousness far from your tent, and place your gold in the dust, and the gold of Ophir among the stones of the brooks, then the Almighty will be your gold and choice silver to you. For then you will delight in the Almighty and lift up your face to God. You will pray to Him, and He will hear you; and you will pay your vows. You will also decree a thing, and it will be established for you; and light will shine on your ways. When you are cast down, you will speak with confidence, and the humble person He will save. He will deliver one who is not innocent, and he will be delivered through the cleanness of your hands." Job 22:21-30

Again, living close to Christ, being guided constantly by the Spirit, and freely offering forgiveness as a way of life is the absolute opposite of easy. We must remind ourselves we live in a world that is not our home and is hostile towards the things of God. If that were not enough, there are times as we progress in our walk, when the Father will test us in order to reveal whether or not we truly have the fullness of God's forgiving nature within us. It may be that we will be reminded of past wounds through a simple phone call during which a name is mentioned; it may be that we surprisingly see a past offender at the grocery store or restaurant; or it may be that they initiate communication after a long absence through email or a social network message. Whatever the case may be, our emotions will point the way to how we are living. If revenge or anger immediately springs up, then we are not living in God's forgiveness. If we would rather flee the situation rather than stay and be cordial, then we have a ways to go in experiencing the fullness of God's forgiving nature.

It matters not what was done to you, the Lord desires everyone to continue processing their wounds towards the truth, until we have received the fullness of His forgiveness, which extends naturally to others. If you need to say to yourself over and over, "This is between me and God. It really does not depend upon them at all." Go ahead and say it. Injustice and wounds inflicted upon you result in the natural response of anger and frustration, which is understandable and allowable. However, God calls us to go towards and offer forgiveness one hundred percent of the time, not based upon what they deserve, but based upon His nature of forgiveness. We will reach the fullness of this forgiveness when we can intercede in prayer on the other party's behalf; and when we are able to ask God to shatter their hardness of heart and spirit, so they may be free to live a life of freedom and joy.

At one of our retreats, we had a couple from out of town. Both the husband and the wife had been previously divorced and been married to each other for about twenty years. Thirty or so years earlier, the wife's ex-husband had kidnapped their daughter and moved to another state. The wife at the time did not have the wherewithal to pursue legal remedies, and thus, lost the ability to have a relationship with her daughter. In recent years, she was able to locate her daughter, now an adult, and made attempts to reconcile the relationship. Her daughter had been poisoned by her father. Because her thoughts about her mother had been horribly tainted by her father, she rebuffed any attempt to even talk together. She requested that her mother leave her alone and never contact her again. The wife held a deep level of bitterness toward her ex-husband, and now toward her daughter, who was not even willing to open up simple communications. She was living under additional pressure of disappointment and resignation (thinking that God was not really good), along with a level of guilt that she did not fight for her daughter when she was kidnapped. There were lots of emotions dominating her soul, resulting in a life of sadness and heaviness. During the retreat, we addressed this whole issue of forgiveness and reconciliation: that God calls us to forgive 100% of the time and 100% of people, including those that have hurt us deeply. The wife recognized that this issue had put her in bondage and was the cause of her deep sadness. She spent time one afternoon in the Scriptures and in the Spirit, allowing God to transform her heart. She fully received His forgiveness and the ability to forgive both her ex-husband and her daughter. On the last day of the retreat, she announced that she had experienced such freedom that she could intercede for both of them - that God would intervene in their lives to reveal to them each His forgiveness and thus a desire to reconcile the relationship with her. During her time of intercession, she heard

God speak to her that He would bring about reconciliation with her daughter. The next day we received an incredible phone call. Having returned back home, the wife received a phone call from her daughter - telling her that she had recently accepted Christ as Lord and Savior. Though she had struggled with her own issue of forgiveness and was not willing to even talk to her mother, God had broken through on Sunday and helped the daughter understand forgiveness and gave her a desire to reconcile. She was prompted to call her mother to set up a time to meet and open the relationship. How cool is that? One of the beautiful truths of God is that he works both sides of every problem - one of the reasons we are to simply live in forgiveness, offer reconciliation, and allow God to do His work to bring about His desire for freedom and reconciled relationships. This was certainly a real example to all of us of the power of forgiveness and the beauty of reconciliation through forgiveness and intercession.

With this real story in mind, are there some painful and/or traumatic events in your past? Regardless of your involvement or guilt for lack of involvement, you might be in bondage to your bitterness and guilt just like this woman was. However, through forgiveness and allowing God to transform your heart, you can be released from all of your past hurts, even the excruciating events, and be set free. Are you willing to let God transform you from the inside out?

CHAPTER 19
MINISTRY OF RECONCILIATION

We have firmly established God's desire to reconcile all people to Himself and His desire for us to show this same behavior to everyone we encounter. Our behavior indeed shows the world how we live and in which kingdom we walk (the kingdom of light or the kingdom of darkness). We are to maintain living in the Spirit by taking to heart everything God has set forth in His Word. We are to cherish the Scriptures and live according to them. We are to flee every appearance of evil and only seek that which is good and profitable. When we live led by God's Spirit, these behaviors are a natural outpouring of a grateful heart and one who truly loves the Lord; and God always takes care of His own. He is mighty to save, and He will save. He is able to deliver His children, and He will deliver them. He does hear his children's pleas, and He delights to answer them. From thankful hearts and the overflow of gladness, we have a job to do in this dying and hurting world. We are called to be ambassadors for Christ and His ministry of reconciliation. Those who have been reconciled are called, even ordered, to tell those who are not yet of God's flock about His forgiving nature, about His freely offered gift, about how to live in peace with their mighty and loving creator. Only those who have received this gift can carry out such a mission, and only those who have received can go out with the undying passion and unrelenting fire needed to take the Good News to the world.

MINISTRY OF RECONCILIATION

"You have heard that the ancients were told, 'You shall not commit murder' and 'Whoever commits murder shall be liable to the court.' But I say to you that everyone who is angry with his brother shall be guilty before the court; and whoever says to his brother, 'You good-for-nothing,' shall be guilty before the supreme court; and whoever says, 'You fool,' shall be guilty enough to go into the fiery hell. Therefore if you are presenting your offering at the altar, and there remember that your brother has something against you, leave your offering there before the altar and go; first be reconciled to your brother, and then come and present your offering. Make friends quickly with your opponent at law while you are with him on the way, so that your opponent may not hand you over to the judge, and the judge to the officer, and you be thrown into prison. Truly I say to relationships. This will not come out of there until you have paid up the last cent."
Matthew 5:21-26

"We are not again commending ourselves to you but are giving you an occasion to be proud of us, so that you will have an answer for those who take pride in appearance and not in heart. For if we are beside ourselves, it is for God; if we are of sound mind, it is for you. For the love of Christ controls us, having concluded this, that one died for all, therefore all died; and He died for all, so that they who live might no longer live for themselves, but for Him who died and rose again on their behalf. Therefore from now on we recognize no one according to the flesh; even though we have known Christ according to the flesh, yet now we know Him in

this way no longer. Therefore if anyone is in Christ, he is a new creature; the old things passed away; behold, new things have come. Now all these things are from God, who reconciled us to Himself through Christ and gave us the ministry of reconciliation, namely, that God was in Christ reconciling the world to Himself, not counting their trespasses against them, and He has committed to us the word of reconciliation. Therefore, we are ambassadors for Christ, as though God were making an appeal through us; we beg you on behalf of Christ, be reconciled to God. He made Him who knew no sin to be sin on our behalf, so that we might become the righteousness of God in Him." 2 Corinthians 5:12-21

"Never pay back evil for evil to anyone. Respect what is right in the sight of all men. If possible, so far as it depends on you, be at peace with all men. Never take your own revenge, beloved, but leave room for the wrath of God, for it is written, 'Vengeance is Mine, I will repay,' says the Lord." Romans 12:17-19

"Therefore, strengthen the hands that are weak and the knees that are feeble, and make straight paths for your feet, so that the limb which is lame may not be put out of joint, but rather be healed. Pursue peace with all men, and the sanctification without which no one will see the Lord. See to it that no one comes short of the grace of God; that no root of bitterness springing up causes trouble, and by it many be defiled; that there be no immoral or godless person like Esau, who sold his own birthright for a single meal. For you know that even afterwards, when he desired to inherit the blessing, he was rejected, for he found no place for repentance,

MINISTRY OF RECONCILIATION

though he sought for it with tears." Hebrews 12:12-17

"Come, you children, listen to me; I will teach you the fear of the Lord. Who is the man who desires life and loves length of days that he may see good? Keep your tongue from evil and your lips from speaking deceit. Depart from evil and do good; seek peace and pursue it. The eyes of the Lord are toward the righteous and His ears are open to their cry. The face of the Lord is against evildoers, to cut off the memory of them from the earth. The righteous cry, and the Lord hears and delivers them out of all their troubles. The Lord is near to the brokenhearted and saves those who are crushed in spirit. Many are the afflictions of the righteous, but the Lord delivers him out of them all. He keeps all his bones, not one of them is broken. Evil shall slay the wicked, and those who hate the righteous will be condemned. The Lord redeems the soul of His servants, and none of those who take refuge in Him will be condemned." Psalm 34:11-22

When we follow Christ, we are called to be His ambassadors. What exactly is an ambassador? It is defined as a diplomatic official of the highest rank, sent by the ruler of a state or country to another state or country as its resident representative or to represent them on a temporary mission. So, God's Word seems to be labeling all believers as God's resident representatives on earth to execute His desires while we are temporarily living on this earth. What desires does God have for His ambassadors to do? Primarily to offer reconciliation to every person we encounter; to show them, to tell them, and to beg them

LIFE IN FORGIVENESS

to be reconciled to God directly. God deeply desires and longs for all of creation to be reconciled to Himself, and when we are walking according to His Spirit, that same desire and longing wells up in each of us when thinking about our friends, family, and co-workers. Having been told over and over again, we know how to walk in the Spirit: abiding in the word, abiding in relationship with Jesus, abiding in prayer. It seems pretty simple, but remember that John 15:5 states how we can do nothing apart from Christ. This includes the desire for others to be reconciled to God, as well as our personal relationship with our Father. We really cannot do anything apart from Him. Reconciliation is not merely resolving an issue between two people or groups. Rather, reconciliation seeks to bring the life of God Almighty into our existing relationships in order to bring freedom, joy, peace, awe and wonder. As we are being led by the Spirit and are doing our best to be at peace with everyone else, we cannot sacrifice the truth for the sake of peace. In no way are we expected to compromise or give in to others merely to avoid conflict, nor are we expected to allow others to continually hurt us. Instead, the expectations put upon us is to have hearts that seek peace and be willing to work at the issue with the other party until a conclusion, preferably one which leads to full reconciliation and peace, is met. Scripture also states how if we have hurt or done something against another and recognize our error during our worship or prayer time, we are to immediately go to them and process through what was done in order to achieve reconciliation. The motivation here is placed upon the believer to process the truth, confess any and all wrong, and to seek a resolution and restoration. If we are the harmed ones and have legitimate anger and frustration, we are to forgive them first and then follow that with an opportunity to discuss the conflict, process through it, and offer peace and reconciliation with our offender.

Offering Reconciliation

Again, how are we to offer reconciliation to others? On the same basis God offers it to us. We must stand on unwavering truth, process through the truth, and refuse to move off our own understanding of truth until a satisfactory resolution has been reached in working towards reconciliation. Somewhere we have heard this before: Forgiving and loving first and then offering reconciliation to God … it reminds us of the cross. So, in the same way Christ offers us forgiveness and reconciliation to the Father through the work done on the cross, we are to offer forgiveness and reconciliation to others. Truth must prevail as we stand firmly rooted in that which has been set forth in God's Word. Processing the hurt and offense done to us is difficult and painful, but we must do so in a way that glorifies God, in truth and love. And we must stay the course until the resolution to the conflict comes, and it leads to reconciliation for both parties.

> *"Make me know Your ways, O Lord; teach me Your paths. Lead me in Your truth and teach me, for You are the God of my salvation; for You I wait all the day… All the paths of the Lord are loving-kindness and truth To those who keep His covenant and His testimonies."* Psalm 25:4-5, 10

LIFE IN FORGIVENESS

"And He gave some as apostles, and some as prophets, and some as evangelists, and some as pastors and teachers, for the equipping of the saints for the work of service, to the building up of the body of Christ; until we all attain to the unity of the faith, and of the knowledge of the Son of God, to a mature man, to the measure of the stature which belongs to the fullness of Christ. As a result, we are no longer to be children, tossed here and there by waves and carried about by every wind of doctrine, by the trickery of men, by craftiness in deceitful scheming; but speaking the truth in love, we are to grow up in all aspects into Him who is the head, even Christ, from whom the whole body, being fitted and held together by what every joint supplies, according to the proper working of each individual part, causes the growth of the body for the building up of itself in love… Therefore, laying aside falsehood, speak truth each one of you with his neighbor, for we are members of one another. Be angry, and yet do not sin; do not let the sun go down on your anger, and do not give the devil an opportunity… Let no unwholesome word proceed from your mouth, but only such a word as is good for edification according to the need of the moment, so that it will give grace to those who hear. Do not grieve the Holy Spirit of God, by whom you were sealed for the day of redemption. Let all bitterness and wrath and anger and clamor and slander be put away from you, along with all malice. Be kind to one another, tender-hearted, forgiving each other, just as God in Christ also has forgiven you." Ephesians 4:11-16, 25-27, 29-32

However, when we truly seek reconciliation with someone who has hurt us, we must be willing to adjust our understanding to their truth.

MINISTRY OF RECONCILIATION

Now, God's truth never changes, and in no way are we to change our understanding or mind according to anything contrary to Scripture. However, our personal truth about what happened within an incident, which includes our perception of intention, what was said, and how we feel must be adjusted to what the other side says about their perception of intention, reception, words said, and how they felt. We must be willing to understand where they are coming from and receive what they have to say to us and about us, regardless of how much it initially hurts. We must be humble enough to confess any wrong or injustice done on our part in response to our wound. If we have contributed to the misunderstanding between the two parties or hurt the other side in any way, we must also ask for forgiveness from them. It is also necessary for us to speak the truth in love. When we approach the conflict with respect and tenderness, the opportunity for reconciliation is genuine. Avoid ignoring the truth for just the appearance of a reconciled relationship. The truth does set us free, and only when the truth is embraced can real reconciliation occur. Again, regardless of how difficult this may be, we must be willing to stay within this process until a heart-level agreement can be made. Stick with it until you fully understand their side, until the negative emotions subside, anduntil freedom comes. Then and only then can conflict be resolved, forgiveness be offered on both sides, and reconciliation and restoration happen. Now, practically speaking, how is this lived out?

Always begin with the Lord, and let His truth guide you into all truth, regardless of the circumstance. From there, we process through the conflict to a resolution.

CHAPTER 20
PRACTICAL APPLICATION PROCESSING

So how does all of this work in everyday life? By way of illustration, I will share a situation that illustrates how this works. I received a phone call one day from a senior executive of a Fortune 500 company, whom I knew as an acquaintance. He said that he knew that I could help people process God's will and wanted to meet for lunch to process through what he believed he was understanding as God's will. At lunch he proceeded to say that he believed God was calling him out of being an executive to serve as a senior preaching pastor – even though he had no formal seminary education or training. I listened respectfully. Having seen him speak publicly before, I did not sense that his gift was preaching. However in seeking God's will, it is not to be based on what we sense but rather on what we hear. So during our conversation, I prayed for God to give me revelation about His will regarding this executive leaving his position to become a pastor. What I heard was "no." It was not God's will, but this executive was seeking his own will. So after asking a few questions, I simply stated that my spirit could not confirm that what he was hearing was God's will, and I encouraged him to seek further to truly hear God's plan. Knowing that God will communicate His desires directly, I understood that it was, and is, not my right to say that God's will was this or that, but rather share the truth of what I heard and either say, "Yes, my spirit confirmed that," or "No, my spirit did not confirm that."

PRACTICAL APPLICATION PROCESSING

Since we, as believers, have the same Holy Spirit, it actually is rather easy to come to agreement and confirmation because the Spirit in us will reinforce God's will collectively. Upon me sharing what I was hearing, this person slammed down his utensils, stormed out, and left me to have lunch alone (and pick up the bill). I was surprised but knew that I had been faithful to what I had heard from God. A few days later, I received a four-page, hand written letter from this executive, accusing me of being worse than an infidel, saying that I didn't know what was doing, that I didn't hear God, and that I should stop assisting anyone in attempting to hear God's will. There was four pages of vituperative accusations against my character, my Christianity, and my relationship with God! Needless to say, I was angry and hurt. This person had called me, and I did not say directly that I disagreed with his understanding of God's will but just suggested that he consider going further. His character assassination on me was inappropriate and certainly not deserved. I sat down and began to write a rebuttal and defense to his accusations. My emotions were high, and I realized that I had unforgiveness toward this person.

First and Foremost – Forgive

"Tremble, and do not sin; meditate in your heart upon your bed, and be still. Selah. Offer the sacrifices of righteousness, and trust in the Lord." Psalm 4:4-5

"Be angry, and yet do not sin; do not let the sun go down on your anger, and do not give the devil an opportunity." Ephesians 4:26-27

LIFE IN FORGIVENESS

"And He said to them, 'When you pray, say: Father, hallowed be Your name. Your kingdom come. Give us each day our daily bread. And forgive us our sins, For we ourselves also forgive everyone who is indebted to us. And lead us not into temptation.'" Luke 11:2-4

Nothing has changed with what has been said. Forgiveness from God is never based upon what we deserve. Neither should we offer forgiveness to others based upon what they deserve. Our anger and subsequent separation from the one(s) who hurt us want to hold onto the animosity and unforgiveness, but we must not give in to their enticing message. We offer forgiveness based upon what God has done on our behalf already, based upon God's nature we have experienced. Forgiving others is to our benefit and necessary to live truly free. The forgiven shall forgive. And not just at an intellectual level, but at the deepest heart level. It is at this level where the very Spirit of God resides and allows us to fully and gratefully appreciate our own forgiveness and thus translate that thankfulness into freely forgiving others.

In the situation with this executive, I first had to go off into communion with the father to resettle my heart and to receive his nature in me about this person: for me to have true forgiveness on the same basis that God gave me and not what this person deserved. What he deserved was to get my anger and wrath and for me to "get him back." However, since forgiveness is between me and God, I had to get my heart back to forgiveness so that I could truly have freedom and the reality of forgiveness in my heart for this person - not as an intellectual step of obedience, but a true forgiveness in my heart.

PRACTICAL APPLICATION PROCESSING

Offer Reconciliation with Respect, Kindness and Honor

"Therefore if there is any encouragement in Christ, if there is any consolation of love, if there is any fellowship of the Spirit, if any affection and compassion, make my joy complete by being of the same mind, maintaining the same love, united in spirit, intent on one purpose. Do nothing from selfishness or empty conceit, but with humility of mind regard one another as more important than yourselves; do not merely look out for your own personal interests, but also for the interests of others. Have this attitude in yourselves, which was also in Christ Jesus, who, although He existed in the form of God, did not regard equality with God a thing to be grasped, but emptied Himself, taking the form of a bond-servant, and being made in the likeness of men. Being found in appearance as a man, He humbled Himself by becoming obedient to the point of death, even death on a cross. For this reason also, God highly exalted Him, and bestowed on Him the name which is above every name, so that at the name of Jesus every knee will bow, of those who are in heaven and on earth and under the earth, and that every tongue will confess that Jesus Christ is Lord, to the glory of God the Father." Philippians 2:1-11

"Therefore, laying aside falsehood, speak truth each one of you with his neighbor, for we are members of one another. Be angry, and yet do not sin; do not let the sun go down on your anger,

and do not give the devil an opportunity. He who steals must steal no longer; but rather he must labor, performing with his own hands what is good, so that he will have something to share with one who has need. Let no unwholesome word proceed from your mouth, but only such a word as is good for edification according to the need of the moment, so that it will give grace to those who hear. Do not grieve the Holy Spirit of God, by whom you were sealed for the day of redemption. Let all bitterness and wrath and anger and clamor and slander be put away from you, along with all malice. Be kind to one another, tender-hearted, forgiving each other, just as God in Christ also has forgiven you."
Ephesians 4:25-32

Scripture tells us our emotions towards everyone should be honoring, respectful, and kind, even and especially to those with whom there is conflict. When these emotions marry the truth, people see God living in us. Our goal is not to just bring about a solution that everyone agrees to and accepts. More importantly, it is to show others and help them realize how walking in the Spirit is a place of immense peace and joy, a place of righteousness, a place of ultimate freedom and wonder. How we offer and discuss reconciliation directly reflects Christ's nature within us, and our opposing party will see that beauty and freedom we have embraced and that we offer to them in turn. However, if we continue to experience emotions of anger or revenge towards another, it simply means we have not forgiven them and are not able to walk in peace and freedom yet. When this is the case, we need to ask ourselves some basic questions:

PRACTICAL APPLICATION PROCESSING

- How does each party see the truth about the situation at hand?
- What resolutions does each side offer regarding this situation?
- Is there a resolution which satisfies each party?
- If so, great! If not, why or why not?

In my example with this executive, having forgiveness in my heart, I was able to call him and say that I received his letter and that I would like to meet again to discuss it all. Because I had forgiveness, I could treat him with honor and respect, even in my request to meet.

At this point, the result is usually clear. Typically the parties involved have either (1) processed the truth of the situation until there is agreement on the resolution, where reconciliation and a restored relationship ensues or (2) attempted to process the truth of the situation that cannot reach agreement on the resolution and remained either partially or completely unreconciled; or (3) they are not willing to process the truth at all and remained completely unreconciled.

When there is an attempt to process truth, but the opposing sides still see things differently – and as of yet, there is no resolution making everyone happy – the best action is to temporarily separate and return to your bed. This means spend time alone (Psalm 4:4-5) and process with the Lord. Continue praying and seeking His voice, forgiveness, and wisdom until you have reestablished true forgiveness in your own heart. Only then do you return to process truth with the other person(s) with respect and tenderness. If a resolution still cannot be reached, we need to continue to stay in forgiveness and asked the Father to provide resolution to the situation and conflict. If both parties are walking in the spirit and know that God will provide a solution, they can continue to respect and honor each other, as they seek to work through truth until a resolution is reached. Forgiveness will characterize each of their hearts, as well as a respectful desire to get to God's truth knowing that God's truth will become known, and then full reconciliation can be reached.

When Disagreements Remain

When opposing parties do not agree and still see things differently; when any discussed resolution is unsatisfactory to either party, there are three possibilities to come to reconciliation:

- My resolution is truth, and God has to change the other party's heart to understand and receive that truth.

- The other party's resolution is truth, and God has to change my heart to understand and receive that truth.

- God reveals a new resolution, as He changes both parties' hearts to understand and receive this new truth.

When we are both living in forgiveness, we understand that one of these possibilities will be revealed to us by God. And since both of us are in humility seeking God's will, we are willing to let God change our hearts, change the other person's heart, or show us something brand new that brings about the answer to reconciliation. This is why it is so easy to stay in the place of forgiveness with a heart

PRACTICAL APPLICATION PROCESSING

toward reconciliation, including my position and my understanding that truth may need to be altered and changed by God to get to the real truth and real reconciliation.

Linda and I owned an investment property that had provided stable cash flow for our portfolio. I had come to a conclusion that it would be a good idea to sell the property and invest in another property. Linda disagreed and did not sense that this was God's will. I felt strongly, so I worked hard to persuade her that this was a good idea. She felt equally as strongly and resisted. We got into a debate and were at odds with each other. Understanding the process of forgiveness and reconciliation, we separated and got our hearts back right with God. As we received forgiveness toward each other, (again on the same basis that he forgive us – by His nature, and not what we deserve), we were then able to come back together and begin processing the truth about what each of us felt about this situation. (The tools we use are described below). We both still had strength of conviction and did not reach resolution. However, because we were in forgiveness, could respect and honor each other and knew God would give us His resolution, we were able to enjoy the day and the weekend following without allowing this disagreement to burden us. We both then went to prayer knowing that God would either change my heart, Linda's heart or show us something new. Over the following week, God showed me that my conclusions were not in sync with His and that the timing for selling this investment property was not to be now. Through a willingness to humbly seek God's will, He changed my heart, and I was willing to accept His answer. I then went to Linda and explained that God had changed my mind and that it was not time to sell, as she had heard. We reached resolution, and were fully reconciled. Interestingly enough, a year later the Lord showed us both that the timing was right for the sale of the property – and it sold at full price in a very depressed market! We both would like to testify that this process is not difficult, rather it is nothing but joy (even when we initially experience anger and hurt – the reason the process is needed), and there is nothing better than seeking and receiving God's will.

In order to process together in order to reach a resolution and reconciliation, the following tools are recommended:

- **How does each side see the truth about this situation?** A good technique to use for this is to have each side share his/her view of what happened. After they have spoken, repeat what they have said and then ask, "Did I understand you correctly?" and "Is there anything else you would like to say regarding the issue?" Return to the beginning and repeat as many times as needed, until both questions are answered positively. Then reverse roles, until you feel as though you have been fully heard and understood.

- **Focus on the actual issue at hand.** Once both sides have been fully heard and understood, often what happens is each party realizes they agree on more than they originally thought. Usually there are only one or two key issues needing to be

PRACTICAL APPLICATION PROCESSING

resolved in the conflict. When you realize the actual issues, focus on those alone and work towards a resolution that will bring about reconciliation.

- **Offer a solution.** Once the key issues have been realized and discussed, each side should take a turn in offering a resolution satisfactory to both parties. First, the resolution would be stated and why it would be reasonable. Next, they would explain what they are willing to do (or not do, whatever the case may be) to resolve the issue. Then the opposing party would ask the same questions as before regarding the resolution such as, "Did I understand you correctly?" and "Is there anything else you would like to say here?" Once they are both positive answers, the other person takes a turn, just as before.

- **Discuss if the solutions are acceptable to everyone.** If they are, fantastic! Agree on the solution, and live in the freedom of a reconciled and fully restored relationship, agreeing to not bring up the conflict again in the future. However, if neither resolution is adequate, more work needs to be done. Remember: the solution to the problem cannot violate Christ's truth. Therefore, the solutions must be truthful, and if they are not, then continue the process until they are. If a truthful resolution cannot be agreed upon, you must be willing to not be reconciled.

The sooner we choose to process the truth, forgive, come to a resolution, and continue down the path towards full reconciliation, the sooner we will reap the benefits of walking in the Spirit: peace that passes all understanding and the freedom that truly sets us free. However, going through the entire process may take some time, which is completely understandable and acceptable. Our role is to make sure that we are living in forgiveness, and let God speak to the other side. Also, make sure you are listening to the other party's side, clarifying along the way as needed, all the while acknowledging their feelings, words, and view of the truth. In addition, continue acting with respect, kindness, and honor towards your offender. However, if you are not being treated with respect and honor, the process may have to cease until respect can be shown on both sides or both parties will have to live not reconciled. If this is being threatened, ask yourself and your offender if you both can set aside the conflict until a later date, but with a continued heart towards resolution. With these attitudes and guidelines practiced, we should be able to live in such a way that a lack of agreement does not ruin our attitudes, our days and nights, or our interactions with others. For this to fully work, a few things must happen on both sides of the conflict:

- **Each party must turn first to forgiveness and remain in forgiveness.** If you are operating in forgiveness, but your offender is not, keep the forgiving mindset. If believers continue to walk guided by the Spirit and remain humble, it creates an environment where it is easier for the other party to process with respect, kindness, and honor.
- **Each party must have a desire to be an ambassador for**

PRACTICAL APPLICATION PROCESSING

Christ and have a ministry of reconciliation. Again, we are only responsible for ourselves. If the opposing person or party has no desire to participate in the ministry of reconciliation, we are to remain ambassadors and continue treating them with respect. The offer to process through the conflict is presented over and over with respect. Each party must be willing to process the truth of the situation and have integrity while doing it.

- **Each party must be willing to process truth – and have integrity about that truth.** You need to continually stand on the truth, share the truth, and never compromise the truth. Just as important is for you to ask the other person(s) to stand on their truth, share their truth, and not compromise their truth. Why? You do not want the other party to give in or cave merely for the sake of resolving or avoiding conflict. When this happens, conflicts are never resolved. Because of this, you need to create a safe environment for them to continue to share what's on their heart, so that a resolution based around truth is truly reached. This is particularly significant for a couple where one party generally will give in just to avoid the conflict. Work hard at this, and you will see the ability to process truth well will lead to a wonderful resolutions and the fulfillment of God's will.

- **Each party must be willing to stay within the process until an agreement is found, and a resolution suitable for both parties is decided.** As far as it concerns you, you are always to be willing to continue the reconciliation process. The other party, due to their lack of forgiveness and bondage to their own soul wounds, may walk away from the process and refuse to process further. Remember, your call is to forgive at all times, but reconciliation is based upon truth. You cannot control the other party's response to that truth. So, if they are not willing to be reconciled, then you have to be willing to let the relationship be unreconciled. But you always having the freedom in forgiveness and a willingness to process again if the other party ever decides they desire to pursue truth with you.

Sometimes things do not work out as we wish. For example, if you are remaining in forgiveness and fully willing to fully process through to a full resolution, the other party will set the level of reconciliation. This level is directly dependent upon their living in forgiveness and willingness to process truth. These levels typically fall into three different categories:

- **Non**e – will not be reconciled at all; there will be no relationship and you will remain separated.
- **Partial** – limited processing of truth; they are not willing to go the depth of the feelings of hurt experienced by you. In addition, they choose not to see that what they have done to hurt you and having such an attitude is unhealthy. They are unable to get the full discussion of resolution which will be satisfactory to you, since they are never able to process the full truth. Such circumstances will typically result in a surface-level

PRACTICAL APPLICATION PROCESSING

relationship; you will spend limited time together and will have boundaries in regards to how much time and in what situations are satisfactory to and healthy for you.

- **Complete** – Fully restored relationship; both of you will experience all the benefits of God's forgiveness:

Each and every step happens and happens seamlessly in an ideal situation. But we do not always find ourselves in ideal situations. However, less than perfect circumstances do not negate how we are to act towards the other person. We are responsible for our own actions, reactions and responses. If you and I walk in forgiveness and are fully willing to work out the conflict, the opposing side decides upon the future of the relationship. They set the level of reconciliation based upon how they walk, and if they are going to live in forgiveness or not. If they choose to withhold forgiveness completely, there will be no reconciliation. The relationship has been severed, and a separation will take place between the two. Some people decide to only partially forgive. In these circumstances, they will process the truth and hurt in a limited fashion. They refuse to plunge the depths of the hurt feelings experienced by both sides and will continue to live so unhealthily. Their refusal to fully process the conflict will result in lack of resolution satisfactory to both sides, since truth is not completely addressed. What typically happens here is that the relationship will continue only at a surface level, and any time spent between the two of you will be rather limited. There will be new noticeable boundaries in place regarding how much time and under what circumstances are comfortable and healthy.

In my example with the executive, upon me making a phone call to offer an opportunity to sit and process what happened between us, the executive shouted that he never wanted to talk to me again and hung up. Having already gone to forgiveness, I remained in forgiveness. Knowing that it takes two parties to reach reconciliation through processing truth together, and having offered to sit and process the truth, I knew there was nothing more for me to do. I did not let this burden me or cause me to develop any roots of bitterness. In fact, I gave no thought about it, except I was reminded by God to intercede for this individual. I periodically saw him at a distance and had no trouble being in the same room with him, saying a friendly hello and asking how he was doing. His answers were always short, and he wanted to quickly depart from being with me. I understood that his anger and un-forgiveness was actually trapping him, and I could actually feel sorry for what had occurred within his soul. This is why I could go to intercession on his behalf. I could neither force him to process with me, nor could I dismiss the truth just for the sake of apparent reconciliation. I was called to carry out what Christ has carried out – complete forgiveness based upon His nature and then an offer of reconciliation - understanding that reconciliation may not be possible because of the inability to process truth.

The goal of all our relationships is to always remain in forgiveness; and then move to reconciliation. When this happens, I believe not only does God Almighty smile, but also the angels in heaven cheer and breathe a contented sigh; for once again do they see the work

PRACTICAL APPLICATION PROCESSING

of the cross manifested in humanity. A fully restored relationship between brothers and sisters just points back to the restored relationship between God and mankind. Full restoration and reconciliation is the aim and goal of all conflict. These circumstances receive all the benefits of God's forgiveness:

- Redemption
- His Righteousness
- His Guidance
- His Joy
- Spiritual Power and Authority
- His Peace
- His Mercy, Kindness and Tenderness
- His Healing
- Restoration from Destructive Patterns
- Satisfaction with Good Things

In my example with the executive, nearly a year went by. I had not experienced any anger or bitterness towards him, nor was I burdened by our break in the relationship. I was living in forgiveness and was willing to process truth through to reconciliation, even though he was not. Then one day I received a phone call from him. He said that he would like to meet me for lunch and talk. Having been in forgiveness, I immediately said sure. This is one of the beauties of forgiveness: when the other party who hurt us decides to process the truth, we are always prepared to join the process, with no anger or bitterness coming with us into the process. At lunch he began with saying he was sorry for what had transpired between us and that he had tried for over a year to become a pastor. He mentioned that God had blocked every attempt, and now he realized he had been seeking his own will and had not really been interested in God's will. Looking back he also realized I had been hearing from God and that it was my role as one of God's holy priesthood to communicate what I was hearing and not to compromise. He admitted that his response was inappropriate and cruel. I shared what I had felt both at the beginning of the process (anger and hurt) and throughout the process (forgiveness and intercession) - but I felt no ill will toward him and was thrilled that he had come to know God's will and was now prepared to follow what God had in mind for his life. We both let it all go, and we were fully reconciled to a positive and healthy relationship. Since that time, he has been called, as an executive, to reach and train churches in amazing recovery ministries and is truly serving as a minister of God. He is just serving in a roll designed for him by God to expand what was on God's heart for the Kingdom.

Throughout this book, we have asked you to address some painful issues in your own life, past hurts, past disappointments, traumas, etc., and have gently led you into the truth of the freedom and love and full life available to you. By now, you have all of the tools and resources to live in forgiveness yourself. You have the ability to offer reconciliation to anyone, regardless of what they have done or may do to you in the future. Remember, you cannot do anything apart from Christ, apart from walking in His Spirit, and apart from Him

PRACTICAL APPLICATION PROCESSING

abiding in you as you abide in Him. The choice to live in freedom and love is always contingent upon you, because God's work has already been accomplished upon the cross – once for us all. As you allow the Holy Spirit to transform your mind, your heart, and your life, you will greatly reap all of the benefits of living in the Kingdom. That life will be everything you have ever wanted, dared to dream of, and more. The choice is your,s and the call to follow Christ in forgiveness and reconciliation is always available to you. Leave behind your past failures, your former pain, and look forward and upward. The questions asked to you from your Heavenly Father is simply and always this:

Why not today? Why not now?

CHAPTER 21
QUESTIONS AND ANSWERS

There are some frequently asked and addressed questions/issues which arise when the topic of reconciliation is broached. Here are a few:

Q: What about justice? Doesn't the injustice of the other party who did the wrong and know what they did to be completely unfair, need to be set straight and punished?

A: *"Let love be without hypocrisy. Abhor what is evil; cling to what is good. Be devoted to one another in brotherly love; give preference to one another in honor; not lagging behind in diligence, fervent in spirit, serving the Lord; rejoicing in hope, persevering in tribulation, devoted to prayer, contributing to the needs of the saints, practicing hospitality. Bless those who persecute you; bless and do not curse. Rejoice with those who rejoice, and weep with those who weep. Be of the same mind toward one another; do not be haughty in mind, but associate with the lowly. Do not be wise in your own estimation. Never pay back evil for evil to anyone. Respect what is right in the sight of all men. If possible, so far as it depends on you, be at peace with all men. Never take your own revenge, beloved, but leave room for the wrath of God, for it is written, 'Vengeance is Mine, I will repay,' says the Lord. 'But if your enemy is hungry, feed him, and if he is thirsty, give him a drink; for in so doing you*

QUESTIONS AND ANSWERS

will heap burning coals on his head.' Do not be overcome by evil, but overcome evil with good." Romans 12:9-21

Again, we are to act contrary to the rest of the world. We are to be ruled by God's Spirit and by forgiveness. If we constantly have in the forefront of our minds how much we have been forgiven and how much we deserve nothing but God's wrath, we will more readily offer forgiveness to those who hurt us. It is a choice. We must choose to live in and live out forgiveness. We are told to honor, respect, and be kind to those who are evil to us. The book of Romans tells us to repay evil with good. It is impossible to do this apart from God living within us, but within this difficulty, we must still choose to believe that injustice will be corrected. God always delivers justice, for He is just and perfectly righteous. His justice will prevail; His justice will be perfect; and it is God's prerogative to exact revenge in His way and in His time.

As we walk in the Spirit and understand the truth of justice, we actually are given a different perspective. Instead of us seeking judgment, we have to have a heart for those to see justice and the truth of God which would lead them to repentance and their own walk led by Spirit. When we intercede on the behalf of lost ones, we are repaying good for evil. We are praying that their hearts would be made new, that the carnal nature and hard hearts would be replaced with life abundant and tenderness only available through Christ. When we pray for non-believers to respond to God's truth, which offers eternal redemption and restoration, we are near the very heart of God.

For example, our son and his wife, who have two boys, experienced a very scary situation. One of the employees of my son's company was terminated by his supervisor. That person found out where my son lived and came to his house demanding to speak to him. His wife answered the door and said he was not home and to please leave. This disgruntled employee forced his way a second time, where she and her two boys were, threatening to harm them because he had been let go. Upon learning this, my son called the local police and was able to secure an injunction against this person ever coming into their home and contacting them at all. Unfortunately, this person violated this injunction and sent numerous threatening letters, which my son and his wife ignored. They were worried, fearful, and very angry, but as believers, they were attempting to not let this burden their lives. However, they both admitted that they had not come to a place of true forgiveness. Then they received a letter stating this former employee had a gun and was going to carry out what was necessary to appease what had happened to him. My son took the letter to the police who then arrested the individual and set a court date for him to appear before the judge. The prosecutor contacted my son and told him they would carry out any sentence that my son recommended within the law. At first my son wanted justice to be served, and he and his wife wanted the court to deliver the longest sentence possible. Nevertheless, we gathered together in what we call "Family Council" and discussed the situation. We first processed whether or not my son and his wife had gone to forgiveness. They had not. We told them before we all could come to God's solution, the necessary first step was to spend time with God until they had reached forgiveness. They did spend the time with God, and both received forgiveness towards this person. Then we spent time looking at justice and what God had to say about justice in Romans 12: 9 – 20. It was clear that it was not our duty to establish justice but to let God have his own vengeance, for "thus saith" the Lord. Since this person was married and responsible for his wife, my son and his wife decided before the Lord to recommended probation, with a clear understanding that another violation would result in jail time. My son went even further and paid for the court costs of the second injunction. The son and his wife have not been burdened nor scared any further and since that time, they have had no threats or contact from this person. They fully understand justice will be served, but that it is up to God fulfilling his call to justice. They understand that they are to let go of any desire to set things straight on their own. This is a very valuable lesson to all of us about the process of forgiveness and allowing God to deal with justice.

Q. What about those who have passed away with no chance for reconciliation?

A: *"The Spirit of the Lord God is upon me, because the Lord has anointed me to bring good news to the afflicted; He has sent me to bind up the brokenhearted, to proclaim liberty to captives and freedom to prisoners; to proclaim the favorable year of the Lord and the day of vengeance of our God; to comfort all who mourn, to grant those who mourn in Zion, giving them a garland instead of ashes, the oil of gladness instead of mourning, the mantle of praise instead of a spirit of fainting. So they will be called oaks of righteousness, the planting of the Lord, that He may be glorified. Then they will rebuild the ancient ruins, they will raise up the former devastations; and they will repair the ruined cities, the desolations of many generations."* Isaiah 61:1-4

"Bless the Lord, O my soul, and all that is within me, bless His holy name. Bless the Lord, O my soul, and forget none of His benefits; who pardons all your iniquities, who heals all your diseases; who redeems your life from the pit, who crowns you with loving-kindness and compassion; who satisfies your years with good things, so that your youth is renewed like the eagle. The Lord performs righteous deeds and judgments for all who are oppressed." Psalm 103:1-6

We still need to process through all of the steps. So, we are to do everything that is within us to forgive and let that forgiveness lead to our healing and the eventual freedom and release from all the hurt. Remember, forgiveness is between you and God and not you and the other party. Even if the other party is deceased, we can still work through to forgiveness for all the hurt and pain that they have cost us. When we reach that level of forgiveness, God then brings us freedom and release from our maintained bondage of anger and bitterness towards the person who is deceased. We can truly let it go and move on to the high calling of Christ Jesus and into the beautiful, abundant life he has planned for us. There is nothing more wonderful than being released from the bondage that has captured us for so many years.

QUESTIONS AND ANSWERS

In our retreats, Linda and I have seen this over and over again, particularly concerning dead parents and siblings. Often parents have abused, abandoned, rejected, or oppressed their children and then died estranged from them. Their children are left to deal with the unforgiveness, anger, and unreconciliation of that relationship. When the children (who are attending our retreats), receive the truth that they can gain freedom from this, they spend time with their Heavenly Father, until they receive and experience this forgiveness. They then continue on their journey to have the ability to forgive their dead parents or siblings. They know that the relationship cannot be reconciled, but the freedom from the burden of the relationship can be realized. It is a wonderful thing to experience to see the yoke being lifted when they reach this beautiful state of forgiveness and freedom.

Q: What about a mother and/or father who have deeply abused or hurt me? What if they are continuing to hurt me?

A: This one is always a very difficult one to process. Our father and mother often have and may continue to hurt and oppress us. Often they use manipulation and/or guilt to achieve their own personal goals with no thought of the impact or emotional scarring it causes in their children's lives. However, God has commanded us to honor our father and mother and the commandment carries with it the promise of a blessing or a curse.

"Honor your father and your mother, that your days may be prolonged in the land which the Lord your God gives you."
Exodus 20:12

LIFE IN FORGIVENESS

""See, I have set before you today life and prosperity, and death and adversity; in that I command you today to love the Lord your God, to walk in His ways and to keep His commandments and His statutes and His judgments, that you may live and multiply, and that the Lord your God may bless you in the land where you are entering to possess it. But if your heart turns away and you will not obey, but are drawn away and worship other gods and serve them, I declare to you today that you shall surely perish. You will not prolong your days in the land where you are crossing the Jordan to enter and possess it. I call heaven and earth to witness against you today, that I have set before you life and death, the blessing and the curse. So choose life in order that you may live, you and your descendants, by loving the Lord your God, by obeying His voice, and by holding fast to Him; for this is your life and the length of your days, that you may live in the land which the Lord swore to your fathers, to Abraham, Isaac, and Jacob, to give them." Deuteronomy 30:15-20

"Honor your father and mother (which is the first commandment with a promise)." Ephesians 6:2

How does this happen? It happens one step at a time and by understanding that we will have to learn how to process the truth of reconciliation, along with the joint command of honoring our father and mother. With other people who are not willing to process to reconciliation, we are actually called to dust off our feet and move forward. However, with fathers and mothers, we do not have that option. Thus the key, as with all of our relationships, is to forgive and release the burden of all the hurts and pain that parents have caused us. Although your mother and/or father may not be willing to process any truth, we are still required to do everything in our power to move the parent/child relationship level of reconciliation from severed to partial. We may have to be resigned to the fact of only having a surface relationship with them, which may be extremely difficult. We are to show nothing but respect, kindness and honor to our parent(s), as commanded by God. And while maintaining honor, establish firm and healthy boundaries with them. Such boundaries are done by:

- Praying for the protection of our heart
- Practice avoiding getting drawn into unhealthy situations
- Avoid responding when our "hot buttons" are pushed
- If there is a time limit, remind yourself that it is only for a short time, and the release will come when the time is over.

According to Scriptures, we are not allowed a complete separation from our parents. However, we are able to have a minimal or partial relationship and then move towards a complete reconciliation if they are willing to process truth. Yet, parents are often not willing to process truth, sometimes if we attempt to process truth it makes the situation even worse. Therefore, we are to work at creating times where we can spend time with our parents in that surface-level relationship and not deal with anything deep or heavy. When they attempt to control or manipulate us, we can just let it roll off our backs and not engage in unhealthy dynamics. At the same time, we are not to subject ourselves to situations which only bring about more hurt. So there will be times when we will have to say no to various opportunities to be together and then come up with alternative solutions. For example, instead of joining your parents for a holiday, like Christmas, you can choose to enjoy your holiday with your immediate family and offer alternative dates to get together and celebrate differently with your parents. Do not take the command to honor your father and mother as a license for your parents to control or manipulate you. Instead, you are to find that place where you can respect and honor them, be with them, spend enjoyable time with them, but not allow the way they have hurt you in the past impact your heart any further.

In the situation that I described at the beginning of the book about my anger and unforgiveness toward my mother, I was able to process through to forgiveness and a modest level of a reconciled relationship with her. Because she was unwilling to deal with the abuse and dominance of attempting to control me, my wife, and her family, we had to establish boundaries that were healthy for us, while still giving respect and honor to my mother. Because holidays were of such importance to our immediate family, we no longer were willing to spend the holidays with my mother. What we did do is establish other weekends where Linda and I would spend time with my mother and her husband (not my father, since they were divorced after Linda and I were married). We were respectful and honorable, not reacting to her continued abuse and control, and worked toward just enjoying our time together. As children, we are called to bring honor to our parents, but this can be done in ways that don't allow them to continue to abuse or manipulate us at the same time. Another boundary that we understood was how my mother did not do well in large family meetings. Therefore, we no longer joined in any large group family gatherings, but rather only in small gatherings with my mother and her husband and possibly another of our siblings. This facilitated a more enjoyable experience and did not create the pressure, which caused my mother to overreact and dominate in unhealthy ways. We came to these boundaries through processing together as a couple before God and praying until we reached agreement as to God's will – which is always to honor our parents, and at the same time, not allow them to continue to hurt us or our children. It worked well, and in the latter days of my mother's life, it actually became sweeter and sweeter.

Q: What about a person who has cut me off from all communication?

A: *"So Jesus said to them, 'Truly, truly, I say to you, unless you eat the flesh of the Son of Man and drink His blood, you have no life in yourselves. He who eats My flesh and drinks My blood has eternal life, and I will raise him up on the last day. For My flesh is true food, and My blood is true drink. He who eats My flesh and drinks My blood abides in Me, and I in him. As the living Father sent Me, and I live because of the Father, so he who eats Me, he also will live because of Me. This is the bread which came down out of heaven; not as the fathers ate and died; he who eats this bread will live forever.' These things He said in the synagogue as He taught in Capernaum. Therefore many of His disciples, when they heard this said, 'This is a difficult statement; who can listen to it?' But Jesus, conscious that His disciples grumbled at this, said to them, 'Does this cause you to stumble? What then if you see the Son of Man ascending to where He was before? It is the Spirit who gives life; the flesh profits nothing; the words that I have spoken to you are spirit and are life. But there are some of you who do not believe.' For Jesus knew from the beginning who they were who did not believe, and who it was that would betray Him. And He was saying, 'For this reason I have said to you, that no one can come to Me unless it has been granted him from the Father.' As a result of this many of His disciples withdrew and were not walking with Him anymore. So Jesus said to the twelve, 'You do not want to go away also, do you?'* John 6:53-67

"A ruler questioned Him, saying, 'Good Teacher, what shall I do to inherit eternal life?' And Jesus said to him, 'Why do you call Me good? No one is good except God alone. You know the commandments, "Do not commit adultery, Do not murder, Do not steal, Do not bear false witness, Honor your father and mother."' And he said, 'All these things I have kept from my youth.' When Jesus heard this, He said to him, 'One thing you still lack; sell all that you possess and distribute it to the poor, and you shall have treasure in heaven; and come, follow Me.' But when he had heard these things, he became very sad, for he was extremely rich." Luke 18:18-23

QUESTIONS AND ANSWERS

"Now after this the Lord appointed seventy others, and sent them in pairs ahead of Him to every city and place where He Himself was going to come. And He was saying to them, 'The harvest is plentiful, but the laborers are few; therefore beseech the Lord of the harvest to send out laborers into His harvest. Go; behold, I send you out as lambs in the midst of wolves. Carry no money belt, no bag, no shoes; and greet no one on the way. Whatever house you enter, first say, "Peace be to this house." If a man of peace is there, your peace will rest on him; but if not, it will return to you. Stay in that house, eating and drinking what they give you; for the laborer is worthy of his wages. Do not keep moving from house to house. Whatever city you enter and they receive you, eat what is set before you; and heal those in it who are sick, and say to them, "The kingdom of God has come near to you." But whatever city you enter and they do not receive you, go out into its streets and say, "Even the dust of your city which clings to our feet we wipe off in protest against you; yet be sure of this, that the kingdom of God has come near." I say to you, it will be more tolerable in that day for Sodom than for that city. Woe to you, Chorazin! Woe to you, Bethsaida! For if the miracles had been performed in Tyre and Sidon which occurred in you, they would have repented long ago, sitting in sackcloth and ashes. But it will be more tolerable for Tyre and Sidon in the judgment than for you. And you, Capernaum, will not be exalted to heaven, will you? You will be brought down to Hades! The one who listens to you listens to Me, and the one who rejects you rejects Me; and he who rejects Me rejects the One who sent Me.'" Luke 10:1-16

LIFE IN FORGIVENESS

Jesus lived in complete forgiveness and offered reconciliation through truth to many. The disciples (in the first part of his ministry, there were over 200 following him) found His words about eating his flesh and drinking his blood to be too difficult. Their mistake was not being willing to process the confusing truth further or inquire as to what Jesus actually meant. If they had done so, Jesus would have explained that He didn't mean to eat His physical body or drink his physical blood; but the life He offered was Himself and that He was the bread of life. However they didn't inquire any further and just left. Jesus allowed them to not be reconciled to Himself and let them leave. In turning to his closest twelve disciples, He asked them if they intended to leave as well. If they would have said yes, He would have allowed them to go, too. Another example here is the rich young ruler who desired to know the key to eternal life. He acknowledged he had performed all the requirements of the law, but when Jesus asked him to take a step of faith to demonstrate what was actually in his heart, he could not. He became sorrowful and left. Again, Jesus allowed him to not be reconciled and let him go. Both of these case studies show us how we are to act. Christ specifically instructs us to offer peace to others. Out of our own forgiveness, we offer an opportunity to others to receive forgiveness and live in God's kingdom through His reconciliation based upon truth. We offer this each and every time we offer reconciliation. If the other party is willing to process the hurt and truth, then we are to continue and stay with it until we reach a solution and reconciliation. If they are unwilling to process reconciliation and our peace, then we are to dust our feet off and move on. However, we should always remember to live with a heart of forgiveness and a willingness to reengage at any time, if they come back at a later date and say they are willing to process truth.

In the situation I described with the executive who had rejected an opportunity to sit down and talk through what happened, I was able to dust off my feet and move forward without being burdened by his actions toward me. Because I was in forgiveness and had "dusted off my feet", when he was willing to come back a year later and process the truth, I eagerly and immediately responded. Being in that position of freedom, (whenever someone who has cut us off from relationship is then willing to get together), our hearts are open and desirous of working toward reconciliation, which is our calling by God. However, if they remain separated from us (their choice), then we can continue to live in freedom and not be burdened by their unwillingness.

Q: What about the person who says they are willing to talk, but are never willing to admit and deal with what they have done to hurt me? What do I do with people who are constantly operating in denial and rationalize their actions?

A: Even though they may not be willing to process any truth, our role is still to move the level of reconciliation from a severed relationship to a partial one, as much as it relies upon us. Just as when we were discussing parents, we must be willing to have only a surface relationship while continuing to treat

them with respect, kindness and honor. Establishing healthy boundaries is also necessary by:
- Praying for the protection of our heart
- Practice avoiding getting drawn into unhealthy situations
- Avoid responding when our "hot buttons" are pushed.
- If there is a time limit, remind yourself that it is only for a short time and the release will come when the time is over.

In the situation I described with my mother, we were never able to deal with what she had done to hurt and abuse me in our family. In fact, if I had attempted to push it, it would only have made things worse and served to separate us further. So, we accepted that we would have only partial reconciliation, where we could not talk much about deep things. In addition, we established appropriate boundaries so that we were not drawn into unhealthy situations for me and my family, all while maintaining the level of reconciliation available to us and not attempting to establish it as an all or nothing relationship.

Q: How do I let myself off the hook?

A: This is perhaps the most interesting and difficult area of forgiveness and reconciliation that encumbers us and keeps us in bondage. Many times we acknowledge our own mistakes and things done in the past causing us to live in guilt and sorrow and knowing we have caused harm or damage to others. However, much of the time we neglect to acknowledge we have caused harm and damage to ourselves. We are suffering the consequences of our choices and the consequences are not pleasant. We know we are the cause of our consequences, and because we are fully aware of our own shortcomings and mistakes, we have moved away from God's will for our lives and expect never to be restored again. These lies keep us in sorrow and resignation, constantly beating ourselves up over our failures. The remedy regarding our own mistakes is no different than if we were dealing with another person: we still go through the process of forgiveness. We are the ones who have to be reconciled to God's truth. We are the ones who must work through the process of forgiveness and reconciliation until we can let ourselves "off the hook" and be fully released from the past. Again, we must remember God's forgiveness is not based on what we deserve but rather on the work Christ has already done in our lives. He has already forgiven us and released us from our past.

"Therefore there is now no condemnation for those who are in Christ Jesus. For the law of the Spirit of life in Christ Jesus has set you free from the law of sin and of death." Romans 8:1-2

All of the truths and benefits listed above still apply to us regarding our own animosity against self. We particularly need to remember how God forgets our sin and the redemption offered is free and freely offered.

"Not that I have already obtained it or have already become perfect, but I press on so that I may lay hold of that for which

also I was laid hold of by Christ Jesus. Brethren, I do not regard myself as having laid hold of it yet; but one thing I do: forgetting what lies behind and reaching forward to what lies ahead, I press on toward the goal for the prize of the upward call of God in Christ Jesus." Philippians 3:12-14

"For I am convinced that neither death, nor life, nor angels, nor principalities, nor things present, nor things to come, nor powers, nor height, nor depth, nor any other created thing, will be able to separate us from the love of God, which is in Christ Jesus our Lord." Romans 8:38-39

We must abide in God's word until the truth that there is now no condemnation in Christ Jesus becomes real to us. Notice that Jesus does not only say that He does not condemn you but that there is no condemnation in Christ Jesus… period. This means that He is not condemning you or me, no one else is condemning you or me, and neither are we to condemn ourselves! We can and should learn that we can completely release the past and just press forward to what God has in store for us next. If we can maintain living in this forgiveness and be fully reconciled to Him and the freedom it brings, then we are in a position for God to restore our lives. We can walk in the beauty of his covenant promises to all who follows Him. We need not live any longer in guilt, for when we do, it is a testimony of how we are not living according to the Spirit, but contrarily to God's very nature. We are called to live in the Kingdom of God, where there is righteousness, peace and joy, freedom, and wonder. This is where

QUESTIONS AND ANSWERS

He will restore to you and me the exceptional life we either lost or walked away from. It is likely that before we are fully able to forgive others, we truly need to process forgiving ourselves. Ultimately, this is how we step into God's light and life, receiving His nature, which allows us to forgive others every time.

We need to process the truth of our relationship to God at all costs. We need reconciliation to God before we can tell others it is possible. We need restoration before others can see the testimony of it in our own lives. We must let go of our past, release it, and choose to live in the truth of God's forgiveness. Then we need to move on, beyond our past, to the high calling of Christ Jesus.

I personally had to work through this most difficult area of forgiveness. As a young executive, I was encouraged to increase our family's wealth through real estate investments. While I was managing a division for a Fortune 500 company, I spent a few hours a week developing a commercial real estate project in a different state: purchased the land, constructed a office building, leased the building, and then sold the building. Along with a few investors, we made an amazing amount of money in a short period of time. I decided I could expand this effort by doing three buildings at once and gaining even more financial gain as a result, particularly since it had been so easy on the first one. My wife, Linda, completely disagreed and felt that something was wrong. She strongly opposed me moving in this direction. Since she could not explain to me exactly why, and I was rather stubborn, I proceeded with making the investments along with some of the other investors' money. This occurred at the beginning of the 1980s when the economy took a big nosedive, and commercial buildings were sitting empty as businesses failed to expand due to the economy.

Remember the Resolution Trust? It was set up by the government to handle all the failed real estate from banks which had loaned money to people that had no wherewithal to cover the shortfalls. I was one of those people. But the empty building and the interest payments still had to be paid, and eventually all of our gain from the prior building, as well as all my personal stock and savings, were depleted with no solution in sight. The banks who owned the loans on the buildings required me to file Chapter 7 bankruptcy and took back the properties, processing the properties through the Resolution Trust. Here I was, a Christian, a seminary graduate, and an executive who had just stubbornly ignored God's will and experienced the consequence of that stubbornness - losing all of our family's financial assets. Though we were able to keep our house, I can still remember the day that the car companies came to pick up my automobiles. I had to purchase them back from the bankruptcy court, along with our furniture and my wife's jewelry, including her wedding ring. Needless to say, I was despondent and filled with grief and guilt. One thing that was interesting was that my wife only once said, "I told you so," and she forgave me. I was also surprised to learn that it didn't matter to our children. The material things that we owned were really of no interest to them; they just cared about us being together as a family. My daughter, Michelle, who was nine at the time, would write on a whiteboard outside of my bedroom every morning a Scripture verse of hope, followed by her daily signature —"It will be all right, Daddy."

QUESTIONS AND ANSWERS

While I could receive their forgiveness, I could not forgive myself or let myself off the hook. This was caused by me, and I deserved what had happened to me. Being encouraged to learn this important issue of forgiving self, every day I would walk with Scriptures about forgiveness and process through my heart and feelings with the Lord. Through the daily time spent processing in the Word, about eight months later it broke for me. God had clearly stated that he had forgiven me, and I had no right to reject this forgiveness in my own life. I was to let go of the past and move on. When it broke and the burden lifted, I again received a life of freedom, moving forward into the beautiful restoration and redemption of God's life for us without care about what had already happened.

I've come to know that God is the God of "now." What has passed is in the past, and He encourages us to fully release the past and walk into the fullness of the abundant life that He has planned for us now. This is particularly true, since He can restore and create new things from our lousy choices and mistakes. It reminds me of the GPS in an automobile. If we go off track, the automobile says make a legal U-turn and get back on track. Often we think we know better, so we continue on our course, off-track. We eventually wind up so far off the original route, that it isn't beneficial to go back to the point where we first went off-track. So the GPS says recalculating and establishes a new route to get us to our desired destination. I believe that God is so sovereign that He is fully able to recalculate and reestablish new paths for us to reach the fullness of life ahead of us. He is not limited by our past mistakes, and the good news is that restoration is always available to us. His only invitation to us is: "How about now?" I fully received that there is now no condemnation for those who are in Christ Jesus, and thus, I no longer need to live in guilt but simply repentance. Then I'm free to move on to the high calling of Christ Jesus. We are called to thoroughly enjoy the beautiful relationship offered to us by our Lord Jesus Christ.

Q: What about marriage: What is our call to reconcile?

A: Marriage is the only relationship where we are called to reconcile all the time, every time, one hundred percent of the time. We are commanded to live in complete unity.

"Behold, how good and how pleasant it is For brothers to dwell together in unity ! It is like the precious oil upon the head, Coming down upon the beard, Even Aaron's beard, Coming down upon the edge of his robes. It is like the dew of Hermon Coming down upon the mountains of Zion; For there the LORD commanded the blessing —life forever. Psalm 133

"How blessed is everyone who fears the Lord, who walks in His ways. When you shall eat of the fruit of your hands, you will be happy and it will be well with you. Your wife shall be like a fruitful vine within your house, your children like olive plants around your table. Behold, for thus shall the man be blessed who fears the Lord. The Lord bless you from Zion, and may you see the prosperity of Jerusalem all the days of your life. Indeed, may you see your children's children. Peace be upon Israel!" Psalm 128

QUESTIONS AND ANSWERS

"Go then, eat your bread in happiness and drink your wine with a cheerful heart; for God has already approved your works. Let your clothes be white all the time, and let not oil be lacking on your head. Enjoy life with the woman whom you love all the days of your fleeting life which He has given to you under the sun; for this is your reward in life and in your toil in which you have labored under the sun. Whatever your hand finds to do, do it with all your might; for there is no activity or planning or knowledge or wisdom in Sheol where you are going." Ecclesiastes 9:7-10

"Two are better than one because they have a good return for their labor. For if either of them falls, the one will lift up his companion. But woe to the one who falls when there is not another to lift him up. Furthermore, if two lie down together they keep warm, but how can one be warm alone? And if one can overpower him who is alone, two can resist him. A cord of three strands is not quickly torn apart." Ecclesiastes 4:9-12

"Therefore if there is any encouragement in Christ, if there is any consolation of love, if there is any fellowship of the Spirit, if any affection and compassion, make my joy complete by being of the same mind, maintaining the same love, united in spirit, intent on one purpose. Do nothing from selfishness or empty conceit, but with humility of mind regard one another as more important than yourselves; do not merely look out for your own personal interests, but also for the interests of others." Philippians 2:1-4

LIFE IN FORGIVENESS

"Therefore I, the prisoner of the Lord, implore you to walk in a manner worthy of the calling with which you have been called, with all humility and gentleness, with patience, showing tolerance for one another in love, being diligent to preserve the unity of the Spirit in the bond of peace. There is one body and one Spirit, just as also you were called in one hope of your calling; one Lord, one faith, one baptism, one God and Father of all who is over all and through all and in all." Ephesians 4:1-6

The relationship of marriage is built upon God's ordained central relationship, that the two shall become one: to move in and live within unity, complete agreement, and oneness. (Gen 2: 18 – 25). In contrast to all other relationships where we are can allow them to not be reconciled to us if they are unwilling process truth, we are called to pursue reconciliation with our spouse all the time and every time, regardless of whether they are willing to process truth or not. We are commanded to remain in forgiveness, to ask them to sit down and process truth in a safe and healthy environment, and then work towards a resolution and solution that are truly acceptable to both. In the majority of situations, it is the tenderness paired with humility which will open heart issues and lead the way to true reconciliation. In this way, the marriage can and will be lived out in the exceptional way God intends. We are not called to give up or dust off our feet at any cost, but rather continually work towards full reconciliation. If for some reason, usually due to past unhealthy patterns of your marriage, the other party is not willing to sit down and work through the truth towards reconciliation, then invite them to go to counseling with a third-party believer who can assist the process in opening up wounds and providing techniques allowing for safe communication. However, there are situations where there is a refusal to go to counseling and a refusal to process anything toward reconciliation. In these scenarios, it is legitimate to separate for a time, but always maintaining a forgiving heart and willingness to process truth. If the other party seeks divorce, we are again called to seek reconciliation with all that is within us, but if they truly desire to file divorce then you are to let them go, as long as you have always approached it with a forgiving and tender heart. This should only be a last resort.

As testimony, my wife and I have been married forty-three years. In the beginning years, we struggled with arguing and debating and considered divorce as a solution. Without fully realizing God's command for marriage, we had a sense that we were to attempt to continue to work at it and learn to reconcile. Until we learned the process of true forgiveness, we were lousy at attempting reconciliation. It was more about negotiation, and since I was a better debater, I could successfully negotiate a win for me the majority of the time. Though she may have lost the arguments, she got me back in other ways by being passive aggressive, withholding intimacy, spending of money, etc. We still were battling and had no real sense of what reconciliation looked like. We existed together but we were not in oneness. After we learned forgiveness, and then understood from Scripture the processes of reconciliation, we were able to come to that complete and whole level of reconciliation. We still have disagreements, we still have moments of anger, and still hurting each other, but because we know that we are called to full reconciliation, we simply follow the process: individual forgiveness toward each other, and then sit down with honor and respect to process the truth until we get a solution. If we do not readily find a solution, we allow ourselves to let it remain as is, continue to enjoy our day, our night, our weekend, and then come back in prayer until God gives us the solution. We choose to remember how simple it is: either he changes my heart, changes my spouse's heart, or shows us something new we both did not understand. His solution and His will are best, and there is none better. We always live in full reconciliation. It is pure joy, and our marriage continues to get sweeter and sweeter.

More resources by Richard T. Case:

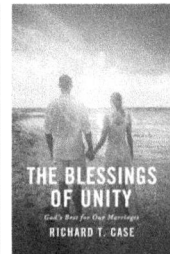

Available wherever fine books are sold!

elevate
publishing

A strategic publisher empowering authors
to strengthen their brand.

Visit Elevate Publishing for our latest offerings.
wwww.elevatepub.com

www.ingramcontent.com/pod-product-compliance
Lightning Source LLC
Chambersburg PA
CBHW070040230426
43661CB00034B/1443/J